BELLINGHAM

MATT AND TOM OLDFIELD

ULTIMATE
FOOTBALL HEROES

BELLINGHAM

FROM THE PLAYGROUND
TO THE PITCH

DINO

First published by Dino Books in 2023,
an imprint of Bonnier Books UK,
4th Floor, Victoria House, Bloomsbury Square, London WC1B 4DA
Owned by Bonnier Books,
Sveavägen 56, Stockholm, Sweden

X @UFHbooks
X @footieheroesbks
www.heroesfootball.com
www.bonnierbooks.co.uk

Text © Matt Oldfield 2023

Design by www.envydesign.co.uk

Paperback ISBN: 978 1 78946 494 8
E-book ISBN: 978 1 78946 502 0

British Library cataloguing-in-publication data:
A catalogue record for this book is available from the British Library.

Printed and bound in Great Britain by Clays Ltd, Elcograf S.p.A.

3 5 7 9 10 8 6 4

For all readers,
young and old(er)

Matt Oldfield is a children's author focusing on the wonderful world of football. His other books include *Unbelievable Football* (winner of the 2020 Children's Sports Book of the Year) and the *Johnny Ball: Football Genius* series. In association with his writing, Matt also delivers writing workshops in schools.

Cover illustration by Dan Leydon.
To learn more about Dan visit danleydon.com
To purchase his artwork visit etsy.com/shop/footynews
Or just follow him on Twitter @danleydon

TABLE OF CONTENTS

ACKNOWLEDGEMENTS

First of all I'd like to thank everyone at Bonnier Books for supporting me and for running the ever-expanding UFH ship so smoothly. Writing stories for the next generation of football fans is both an honour and a pleasure. Thanks also to my agent, Nick Walters, for helping to keep my dream job going, year after year.

Next up, an extra big cheer for all the teachers, booksellers and librarians who have championed these books, and, of course, for the readers. The success of this series is truly down to you.

Okay, onto friends and family. I wouldn't be writing this series if it wasn't for my brother Tom. I owe him so much and I'm very grateful for his belief in me as an author. I'm also very grateful to the rest of my family, especially Mel, Noah, Nico, and of course Mum and Dad. To my parents, I owe my biggest passions: football and books. They're a real inspiration for everything I do.

Pang, Will, Mills, Doug, Naomi, John, Charlie, Sam, Katy, Ben, Karen, Ana (and anyone else I forgot) – thanks for all the love and laughs, but sorry, no I won't be getting 'a real job' anytime soon!

And finally, I couldn't have done any of this without Iona's encouragement and understanding. Much love to you, and of course to Arlo, the ultimate hero of all. I hope we get to enjoy these books together one day.

CHAPTER 1

A DREAM WORLD CUP DEBUT

21 November 2022, Khalifa International Stadium

As the England players walked out onto the pitch
in Qatar, their captain Harry Kane led the way,
followed by experienced goalkeeper Jordan Pickford
and centre-back Harry Maguire. And there, right at
the back of the line, was Jude Bellingham, England's
bright young midfield star.

The boy from Birmingham was about to make his
World Cup debut – wow, what a massive moment
for the nineteen-year-old! So, was he feeling nervous?
No, not nervous – instead, Jude looked calm and

focused on the outside, although on the inside, he was buzzing with excitement. He couldn't wait for kick-off; this had been his dream since he was six years old.

'Let's goooooooooooo!' he clapped and cheered when the national anthems ended.

With Declan Rice sitting deeper in defensive midfield, Jude would have the freedom to get forward for England, just like he did for his club, Borussia Dortmund. That's when he was at his best: running box to box, using his energy and skill to help his team to win.

England's World Cup hero: that's what Jude really wanted to be. He had got his first senior international assist during his player-of-the-match performance against Germany back in September, but his first senior international goal? No, he was still waiting for that…

For England's first twenty minutes against Iran, Jude was a little too eager and excited. He couldn't help it; he was making his World Cup debut! He charged around the pitch like a kid in a sweet shop, taking slightly heavy touches and giving away fouls in dangerous areas.

'Sorry!' he apologised to his England teammates.

As the first half went on, however, Jude settled into the game and got on the ball more often.

PING! He played a midfield-splitting pass through to Mason Mount.

PING! He chipped a lovely long ball out to Kieran Trippier on the right wing.

Yes, with the football world watching, Jude was getting better and better, and so were England. Harry Maguire passed it forward to Mason, who laid it back to Raheem Sterling, who played it out left to Luke Shaw. Much better!

Meanwhile, in the middle, Jude was on the move, running into the gap between the Iran midfield and defence. As he entered the box, he was still unmarked, and so when Luke looked up to cross the ball in, Jude suddenly sprinted forward from the penalty spot.

'Yessssss!'

Jude watched the ball carefully as it floated towards

him and then jumped up at just the right moment to meet it with his head. He had done the first part perfectly; now, for the second part: scoring. Calmly and cleverly, he guided the ball into the corner of the net. 1–0!

Goooooooooooooooooooooaaaaaaaaaaaaaaaaalllllllllllll lllllllllll!!!!!!!!!!!!!!!!!!!

Hurray, England were winning and Jude was their hero, with a goal on his World Cup debut! Throwing his arm around Mason's shoulders, he raced over to the fans to celebrate. But while everyone else around him went wild, Jude didn't even smile. No, he kept his game-face on; they hadn't won yet.

By half-time, however, it looked like England were going to win. First, Bukayo Saka fired in from the edge of the area, and then in injury time, Jude pounced on a loose ball and dribbled forward at speed. After escaping past one defender, he poked a smart pass through to Harry Kane, who crossed it in for Raheem to volley home. 3–0!

What an exciting start for England! As he rushed over to join Harry and Raheem, Jude was enjoying a dream World Cup debut.

Job done, time to slow down? No way – in the second half, Jude was as energetic as ever. He battled for every ball, making lots of important tackles and interceptions in midfield. And when England attacked, he burst into the box in case the cross came in – but this time Bukayo decided to go for goal himself instead. 4–0!

'Get innn!' Jude roared, punching the air with pride.

Despite the scoreline, he was still disappointed when Iran broke through and grabbed a goal of their own. Arghhhh, he had wanted a clean sheet as well as a win. Oh well, never mind, England soon went up the other end and Marcus Rashford scored one more. 5–1!

Time to relax? No – even though their victory was now secured, Jude kept going until the very end. In the eighty-ninth minute, Marcus flicked the ball on, and there was Jude flying in ahead of two opponents to reach it first. With a stretch of his left leg, he played a pass through to Callum Wilson, who cut it back to

Jack Grealish. 6–1!

Okay – now it definitely was game over! Moments later, when the final whistle blew, Jude slowed down and let his game-face drop at last. Job done! He walked around the pitch with a big smile on his face, giving handshakes to his opponents and hugs to his teammates.

'Mate, what a night!' Jude said to Bukayo as they stood there together in the Khalifa International Stadium, soaking up the special atmosphere.

England were off to an excellent start at the 2022 World Cup, and so was their young midfield maestro. One goal, two key passes, plus lots of other great runs, touches and tackles – not bad for a kid who had been playing for Birmingham City in the Championship a few years earlier! After the match, Jude was the talk of all the famous football pundits on TV.

'We're talking about a special, special player here,' marvelled Micah Richards.

'At his age, he's only been playing the game a couple of years,' added Rio Ferdinand. 'It's ridiculous.'

Alan Shearer summed it up perfectly: 'It was a complete performance from a really exciting player.'

What a rapid rise it had been for Hagley's young hero! And the most exciting thing for England was that Jude was only just getting started.

CHAPTER 2

HAGLEY'S NEXT FOOTBALL HERO?

'Dad, Dad!' Jude cried out from the sidelines as the two teams walked out onto the pitch.

At the sound of his young son's voice, Mark turned and gave him a big smile and a wave. 'Hi, Jude! Are you ready to see me score a goal today?'

'YESSSSSSSSS!'

From Monday to Saturday, Jude's dad worked very hard as a policeman, helping to keep their county, the West Midlands, safe. Then on Sundays, he turned into a different kind of hero – a football hero! Sadly for Jude, the job didn't come with a cool mask or cape, but his dad did wear a shirt with black and gold stripes, as well as special shoes with studs on.

Mark Bellingham was a sharp-shooting striker, who had scored lots of goals for lots of non-league teams in the local area: Halesowen Town, Sutton Coldfield Town, West Midlands Police, Bromsgrove Rovers, Stourbridge, and now, for the 2008–09 season, Leamington. The club played in Division One Midlands of the Southern League, seven levels below the Premier League.

Leamington was a forty-minute drive away from their home in Hagley, Birmingham, so Jude didn't always get to watch his dad play. However, if it wasn't raining and if he had been a good boy that week, he often went along with his mum and younger brother, Jobe. The crowds were never very large at the New Windmill Ground, but the fans who did turn up always made as much noise as possible:

And it's super Leaming,
Super Leamington Brakes,
They're by far the greatest team the world has ever seen!!!

Although it wasn't anything like Anfield or Old

Trafford, for a five-year-old boy who was still new to the world of football, the atmosphere sounded really loud and exciting.

'Go on, Dad!' Jude joined in happily from the stand.

FWEEEEEEEEET – time for kick-off!

Jude soon found that the football in the Southern League was quite different from the Premier League highlights he had seen on *Match of the Day* with his dad. There was less skilful dribbling, and more hoofing and heading; less calm passing, and more pushing and kicking.

'Ref, that's a foul!' the Leamington fans yelled angrily each time one of their players fell down on the bumpy, muddy ground.

'Come on, Dad,' Jude muttered to himself, as he shook his restless legs. When was he going to score, like he said he would?

For a lot of the match, Mark didn't move around very much up front. No, fast running wasn't really his striker style. Instead, he waited alertly for the ball to arrive in the opposition box. Then suddenly he sprang into action:

BANG!

*Goooooooooooooooooooaaaaaaaaaaaaaaaalllllllllll
llllllllllllllll!!!!!!!!!!!!!!!!!!!!*

Hurraaaaay! Jude threw his arms in the air and jumped up and down with joy. Leamington were winning, and his dad was the hero!

As the game went on and the score stayed stuck at 1–0, Jude got a bit bored and hungry, but then later in the second half...

THUMP!

*Goooooooooooooooooooaaaaaaaaaaaaaaaalllllllllll
llllllllllllllll!!!!!!!!!!!!!!!!!!!!*

Woah, his dad had done it again. First, a fierce shot and now a powerful header – what a GOAL MACHINE!

'That's my dad!' Jude boasted proudly to all the Leamington fans celebrating around him. By the end of the season, 'Bello' had scored forty-seven goals in forty-seven games, firing Leamington into the Southern League Premier Division for the first time in twenty-four years.

So, would Jude follow in his father's footsteps and one day become Hagley's next football hero?

Mark did his best to kick-start his son's playing career. When he heard that a man called Phil Wooldridge had set up some kids' football sessions in the nearby town of Stourbridge on Saturday mornings, he agreed to help with the coaching, and took Jude along. Each session began with fun kids' games such as cat and mouse, four corners, and capture the bib. At first, that was always Jude's favourite bit. And his least favourite bit? When the footballs came out!

'Aww, do we have to?' Jude moaned, his shoulders slumping. Despite his dad being a football hero, Jude wasn't that interested in scoring goals yet; at the age of five, he just wanted to run around and play the fun kids' games. And if a ball was involved, then he'd rather pick it up and throw it than kick it.

'Look, if you're not enjoying it, that's fine,' his mum said one day when he came home in another bad mood. 'I can tell your dad to stop taking you along.'

But thankfully, Jude didn't give up on football that quickly. Instead, he kept going, and the more Stourbridge sessions he went to, and the more goals he watched his dad score for Leamington, the more he wanted to play the game himself. By the age of six, something had clicked and Mark's plan had worked; Jude had caught the football bug.

CHAPTER 3

HOURS (& HOURS) OF FOOTBALL FUN

'Errr, excuse me, Mr Williams?' a polite voice called out from the doorway.

'Yessssss?' the Hagley Primary School caretaker answered from his desk, without even turning around. He didn't need to; he already knew who would be standing there: Jude. And Mr Williams also already knew what the problem would be: his ball was on the roof, and he wanted it back. Again! Jude came to see him so often that he had started leaving the ladders out ready for the job.

'Right, where is it this time?' the caretaker said, getting up from his chair with a sigh. As he walked over, however, there was a smile on his face because although the boy was always asking for his help, he always asked nicely. Plus, young Jude was showing signs of becoming an excellent player, if he could just learn to keep his shots a bit lower…

'It was Billy's fault, really,' Jude argued passionately, pointing out the part of the roof where he thought the ball had landed. 'My shot was definitely going in until it flicked up off his leg!'

'Hmmm, sure…'

Now that Jude had caught the football bug, there was no stopping him. Before school, after school, break-time, lunchtime – he was always the first one out on the playground, eager to get a game started.

'Hurry up, we don't have long before next lesson!'

Out on the Hagley Primary playground, Jude wasn't a sharp-shooting striker like his dad. He didn't just want to stay up front and score goals. Boring! He wanted to be like his England heroes, Steven Gerrard and Wayne Rooney, running everywhere, and doing everything: passing, tackling, dribbling, shooting. Wherever the action was, that's where Jude wanted to be, battling hard for the ball.

'Pass it – I'm free!'

'Jude's ball!'

'Toby, go go go – make the run!'

'Yesssss mate, that was magic. Rooney, eat your heart out!'

While Jude always wanted to be on the winning team, for now football was still all about fun. Hours and hours of football fun.

When they weren't playing together in school, Jude and his friends from Hagley Primary were playing together out of school, for their first football club. Wooldridge's kids' training sessions had proved so successful that Jude had decided to form a proper team: Stourbridge Juniors. They played in red and white stripes, and who was the other coach who had helped to set the team up? Leamington's legendary striker, 'Bello', of course, or as Jude liked to call him, 'Dad'.

So, what was it like being a manager's son – exciting or embarrassing? Fortunately, Mark wasn't the kind of pushy parent who tried to coach his son all the time. At home, they practised passing together whenever Jude asked to, which was most of the time.

Left foot, right foot, left foot, right foot...

But at Stourbridge Juniors, Mark kept his pre-match messages short and simple:

'Go out there and have fun, and try your best.'

'Play with a smile and give it 100 per cent.'

Yes, Dad! Jude always enjoyed playing for Stourbridge Juniors because although the games were competitive, he was just having a laugh with his mates, doing what he loved most.

'Pass it – I'm free!'

'Jude's ball!'

'Toby, go go go – make the run!'

'Woah mate, what a goal – when did you become Stevie G?!'

Winning certainly helped to make football feel even more fun. By the time Jude was in Year 6, Hagley Primary team had the best team in not only Birmingham, but the whole West Midlands! They made it all the way to the Nationals, which took place at the training ground of top Premier League team, Aston Villa. Jude couldn't wait to go and compete against other schools from all across the country.

'Come on, we can win this!' he told his teammates. Even at the age of eleven, he was already acting like a leader.

Despite all their hard work and togetherness, however, the tournament ended in bitter disappointment for Hagley Primary. They were knocked out in the group stage in the most painful way possible: on goal difference.

'One goal – we lost out by one stupid goal!' Jude groaned afterwards, throwing his head back in frustration. He couldn't believe it; he was absolutely gutted.

Fortunately, however, his despair didn't last long. Soon, he was back to having fun with his friends. Hours and hours of football fun.

'Come on, guys, quick – NEXT GOAL WINS!'

And football wasn't the only sport that Jude enjoyed at Hagley Primary; he played cricket too. In Year 5, he tried out for the school team and didn't quite make it, but he didn't just stop and stick to football. He was too determined to do that. So instead, he worked hard on his cricket skills over the summer with his dad, and when he came back the next year, he was one of the best players in the school. He even helped lead the team to a second National finals!

When Jude's happy time at Hagley Primary came to an end, he had to write an entry for the leavers book, answering statements including, 'When I grow up I want to be...'

Easy! He definitely knew what to put for that one:

'...a professional footballer and play for England.'

To some, that might have sounded unrealistic, but not to Jude or to anyone else at Hagley Primary. Because by then, he was already well on his way to making that dream come true.

CHAPTER 4

BECOMING A BLUE

Despite his love for his teammates, Jude didn't stay at Stourbridge Juniors for long. In fact, he didn't even make it beyond the Under-7s! Because after destroying team after team with his speed, skill and determination, word soon spread amongst the local football scouts.

Have you heard about that Bellingham kid? Yeah, Mark's son, plays for Stourbridge. Well, he scored ten goals last weekend, and another eight the weekend before. And he's meant to be a midfielder!

In 2010, there were four big Midlands clubs flying high in the Premier League:

Aston Villa,

Wolverhampton Wanderers,

West Bromwich Albion,

And Birmingham City.

It was Birmingham who came calling first, but strangely, the club first spotted Jude's talent not at a Stourbridge match, but at one of his dad's Leamington matches.

It was a big game at the New Windmill Ground, and because it was a Sunday morning, not a Saturday, Jude was able to be there with his mum and brother, to watch his dad play. Well, the idea was to watch, but he was way too excited and energetic to stand still for long. If there was a football match going on, then he wanted to be involved!

So after running up and down the sidelines for a while, Jude decided to sneak under the barriers, and out onto the pitch.

'Dad, please can I join in with the warm-up?' he asked and then begged.

'Okay, fine – one shot, Jude,' Mark gave in eventually, 'but then you've got to go back to your mum and Jobe. Deal?'

'Deal!' Jude agreed with glee.

Perhaps the Leamington goalkeeper would have let a seven-year-old score anyway, but Jude's strike was powerful and accurate, skidding low into the bottom corner.

Goooooooooooooooooooaaaaaaaaaaaaaaaallllllllllll llllllllllll!!!!!!!!!!!!!!!!!

'Great shot, Jude!' Mark told his son once he'd finally finished celebrating. 'Now, off you go – the game's about to start.'

'Okay, bye Dad – good luck!'

Also in the Leamington crowd that day was Simon Jones, the Head of Academy Player Recruitment at Birmingham City. He was there to watch the players out on the pitch, but in the end, it was the young boy with endless energy on the sidelines who really caught his eye. It was easy to see that he was a natural athlete and a good footballer too. So, which youth team did he play for? Jones was curious to find out.

'I want someone to go and watch him play,' he told his team of talent-spotters.

Yes, Boss! That day, Jude didn't know that a Birmingham scout was watching him, but it didn't matter because he still put on another all-action performance. One minute, he was sliding in to make a perfectly timed tackle, and the next he was dribbling his way past defender after defender, before sliding the ball into the bottom corner.

Goooooooooooooooooooaaaaaaaaaaaaaaaalllllllllllll llllllllllll!!!!!!!!!!!!!!!!!!!!!

'Well done, Jude!' shouted the Stourbridge Juniors coaches, and not for the first time, or the last, during that match.

'Wow!' In his job, the Birmingham scout saw lots of skilful kids, but what he was looking for was young players with something special, who could do something a bit different on the football pitch. And Jude definitely had that extra 'Wow!' factor. At the end of the match, the scout introduced himself to Mark and invited Jude to come down for a trial with the Birmingham pre-Academy programme.

'What do you think – do you want to go along?' Mark asked his son on their way home.

As a seven-year-old, Jude still saw football as something he did for fun with his friends; he wasn't thinking about playing the sport seriously. Training with a Premier League team did sound pretty cool, though.

'Yeah okay, I'll give it a go,' Jude told his dad, even though he wasn't that excited about joining Birmingham City. Not yet anyway...

'Right everyone, listen up – we have a new player joining us today,' the coach, Mike Dodds, announced at the start of the Under-8s session. 'This is Jude, and I want you all to make him feel really welcome.'

As all eyes turned to look at him, Jude wondered if he was making a big mistake. 'No, I want to stay at Stourbridge!' he thought to himself. There, his teammates were his best friends, whereas here at Birmingham, he didn't know anyone! He was the new kid, and that made him feel nervous and awkward. Oh well – at least he was about to play football, his favourite sport...

During all the training drills and small-sided games, Dodds watched Jude closely. So, was the boy in the fake Barcelona shirt and basic, black boots any good? Yes, he could certainly play. He was speedy, he was skilful, and he could pass and shoot well with both feet. Was he the best player on the pitch? No, not yet, but he definitely had potential, and hopefully with the right coaching Birmingham could help him get there.

By the end of the session, Dodds had made up his mind about his young trialist. 'Well done today,' he said. 'So what do you think – fancy becoming a Blue? We'd love to have you here.'

Jude nodded, a smile spreading across his sweaty face. 'Yes please!'

CHAPTER 5

THE BRILLIANT BELLINGHAM BROTHERS

Before long, there would be two Bellinghams at the Birmingham City pre-Academy. Yes, surprise, surprise – his younger brother, Jobe, had caught the football bug too.

'Jude, get up – let's go out and play!'

Jobe was two years younger than Jude, and now, at the age of five, after spending a lot of time watching his dad and older brother shine on the pitch, he was desperate to become the next star footballer in the family. To put all of his learning into practice, however, he was going to need his brother's help.

'Fiiiiiiiiine,' Jude grumbled, slowly lifting his sleepy head off the pillow, 'but you're going in goal first.'

'Okay, but when you score three, we switch!'

Wearing their best Birmingham football kits and armed with a ball and a pile of cones, the Bellingham brothers headed out onto their favourite patch of grass near their house in Hagley. There, they had all the space they needed to mark out a pitch and two sets of posts, and play safely together for hours. If Denise wanted her sons, she knew exactly where to find them. Day or night, sunshine or rain – they were too focused on football to really care about the weather, and their energy and enthusiasm was endless.

'Jude, should I make this goal a bit bigger?' Jobe asked, looking at the cones he'd just laid down.

His big brother shook his head and smiled. 'Nah, that's big enough for me to score against you, bro!'

'Go on then!' Jobe grinned back, spreading his arms out wide.

Challenge accepted! Jude ran up to the ball and struck a powerful right-foot shot that flew straight past Jobe before he could even dive.

Goooooooooooooooooooooaaaaaaaaaaaaaaaallllllllllllll lllllllllllll!!!!!!!!!!!!!!!!!!!

'Obafemi Martins has surely scored the winning goal for Birmingham City!' Jude cheered as he recreated the striker's celebration from the 2011 Carling Cup Final against Arsenal. Well, the first part anyway. A cartwheel he could do, but a double front flip? No chance.

Since joining the club's academy, Jude had become an even bigger 'Bluenose'. That's what they called the most passionate Birmingham City fans. Near St Andrew's Stadium, there was a famous statue of a face turned sideways and someone had painted the nose blue. On matchdays, Jude always asked his mum and dad if they could walk past it for good luck.

Back on their pitch in Hagley, Jobe wasn't happy.

'Hey, I wasn't ready yet!' he protested, before racing off to get the ball back. That was the problem with not having proper goals with nets, but the Bellingham brothers didn't mind doing a bit of extra running. If their dad wasn't working, he often joined them for a kickaround, but if not, it was just Jude vs Jobe, all day long.

'Right, let the games begin!'

Their football sessions usually started out nice and friendly, with some passing and shooting:

'Bro, you're getting really good!'

'Thanks Jude – do you think I could play for Birmingham too one day?'

'Yeah for sure – together we're going to win loads of trophies!'

…but once they moved on to 1 vs 1 battles, that's when things got less calm and a lot more competitive, especially as they got older and Jobe got better and better. Forget the World Cup final; this was the only match that really mattered! Jude vs Jobe – they were both totally determined to win and prove they were the best Bellingham brother at football.

As the games went on and one of them – usually Jude at first – got closer and closer to victory, they argued over absolutely everything: what the score was, whether a shot was 'in' or 'over' the imaginary crossbar, whether a tackle was fair or a foul…

'Hey, you can't do that – free kick to me!'

'No way, Jobes, I'm just stronger than you!'

'Stop cheating!'

'Stop being a baby!'

'MUUUUUUUUUUUUUUUUUM!'

'Oh come on, boys – what happened this time? If you can't play together nicely, then you shouldn't play together at all.'

But while their football games often ended in fights and tears, they could never stay angry at each other for long. The next day, they always made up and went back to being best friends again.

'Jude, get up – let's go out and play!'

Through all their fierce battles on the local football pitch, the Bellingham brothers pushed each other on to improve, and it was working. Jobe soon got his wish and joined Birmingham's pre-Academy. Jude, meanwhile, was now playing for the Under-10s and building a strong reputation as the club's rising star.

CHAPTER 6

BIRMINGHAM'S NEXT BIG THING

Jude might not have been the best player on the pitch when he first arrived at Birmingham City as a seven-year-old, but he soon was. Once he'd settled in at his new club and started playing proper games for the Under-9s, there was no stopping him. It was like his days at Stourbridge Juniors all over again. Jude was everywhere, running the game from midfield and grabbing goal after goal, and assist after assist.

'It's like he's just gliding across the grass without a care in the world!' his coaches marvelled. 'He makes the game look so easy.'

But what about the next season when Jude moved up to the Under-10s – would he still be able to shine so brightly? Oh yes, in the older age group, he was just as good, if not better!

With a burst of speed and some splashes of skill, Jude dribbled the ball forward, past one defender and then another. Approaching the opposition box, he faked to shoot with his left foot, and then cleverly switched it across to his right. BANG!

Gooooooooooooooooooooaaaaaaaaaaaaaaaallllllllllll llllllllllllll!!!!!!!!!!!!!!!!!!!!

As he received the ball on the halfway line, Jude saw two players rushing towards him. No problem! He calmly shifted it away from the first and then slid it through the second opponent's legs – NUTMEG! This time, he did shoot with his left foot, and the result was the same.

Gooooooooooooooooooooaaaaaaaaaaaaaaaallllllllllll llllllllllllll!!!!!!!!!!!!!!!!!!!!

Wow! That's when Birmingham began to think they might have found their next stand-out star. It had been a very successful spell for the club's academy. First, they had produced goalkeeper Jack Butland, who was now the Number One for the first team, and then two exciting wingers: Nathan Redmond and the new whizz-kid on the scene, Demarai Gray.

All three were talented England youth internationals, but the Birmingham coaches believed that Jude could go on to be even better. So, how were they going to help him to make the most of his phenomenal football talent?

The club wasn't really worried about Jude getting big-headed; he had always been a humble, hard-working kid and his close-knit family would keep him focused and grounded. What the Birmingham Academy coaches were more worried about was him getting bored.

'We just need to come up with special ways to keep challenging him,' they all agreed. That meant sometimes giving Jude more difficult drills to do in training, but also getting him to play against bigger and better opponents.

'We think you're ready to move up to the Under-11s,' the Birmingham Academy bosses told Jude at a meeting with his parents.

What? *Nooooo!* At first, Jude really didn't want to go. He was happy where he was, having fun playing football with his friends his own age. If he joined the Under-11s, he would be the new kid again, plus the youngest member of the team, and he wouldn't know anyone!

But after watching Jude score fifteen goals in the first half of an Under-10s match, the Birmingham coaches decided to try again.

'Look, I know you're having fun here, but you're not going to get any better by scoring loads of goals against kids your own age. You need a new challenge.'

Fiiiiiiiiine! Eventually, Jude agreed and it turned out to be an excellent decision. On his Under-11s debut against Nottingham Forest, he was Birmingham's best player and even scored two goals.

'Okay, maybe you were right!' Jude joked with his coaches.

Before long, he was on the move again – from the Under-11s to the Under-12s, then up to the Under-14s, where his new manager was… Mike Dodds!

'Hello, good to see you again!' the coach said with a smile. 'Ready to work hard and win?'

'Yes, Boss!'

Now that Jude was always playing in the age group above, he was usually one of the smallest boys on the pitch. In the middle of midfield, his opponents often towered over him, but he never let that bother him. Thanks to all those years watching his dad play non-league football, Jude had the grit and determination to battle for every ball. He also had the confidence to come out on top, and the body swerves and drag-backs to lead his team forward on the attack.

'Great work, Jude – keep going!' Dodds clapped and cheered on the sidelines. Wow, the kid had come a long way since he'd first met him as a little seven-year-old! Now, he was the complete midfielder who could do it all – tackle, run, pass, dribble, shoot. But what was his best position on the pitch?

'I think you have the ability to play all areas of midfield,' Dodds told his young star, and what he meant by that was:

Number 4, the holding midfielder, like Arsenal legend Patrick Vieira or Chelsea's Claude Makélélé,

Number 8, the box-to-box midfielder, like Jude's

childhood hero Steven Gerrard,

And. . .

Number 10, the goalscoring playmaker, like his other hero Wayne Rooney.

'There's no reason why you can't do all three roles at the same time. So 4 plus 8, plus 10, equals...'

'Twenty-two,' Jude answered eagerly, like he was back in Maths class.

'Twenty-two,' Dodds repeated. 'Right, from now on, that's your shirt number.'

Jude's eyes lit up – 'Cool, thanks Coach!'

By then, Jude's days of just playing football for fun were over. Now, he was dreaming big. Although he was still working hard at Priory School – his parents made sure of that – he could see his future as a professional footballer paved out in front of him. One day, he was going to become a world-class superstar like Gerrard and Rooney. He was going to play in the Premier League and in World Cups for England.

First things first, however – he needed to keep progressing towards the Birmingham City first team. 'If you want something, put in the hard work and go and get it' – that's what his parents had always said to him. Step by step, Jude was determined to get there.

One day at the academy, he was lucky enough to meet an inspiring football legend. As well as being Britain's first-ever £1-million player, Trevor Francis had also scored the winning goal in the 1979 European Cup final for Nottingham Forest. But before all that, back in 1970, Francis had started his career at Birmingham, becoming the club's youngest-ever player, at the age of sixteen years and 139 days. It was a record that had stood ever since.

Hmmm, interesting! To most people, the idea of making your first-team debut at sixteen years old sounded impossible, but not to young Jude, Birmingham's Next Big Thing.

'I'm going to break that record!' he decided, with no doubt in his mind.

CHAPTER 7

IF YOU'RE GOOD ENOUGH, YOU'RE GOOD ENOUGH

'Are you sure he's ready for this?' Steve Spooner, the Birmingham Under-18s coach, asked. He had welcomed lots of fifteen and sixteen-year-olds into his squad in the past, but a small, skinny fourteen-year-old?!

Dodds, however, nodded back confidently. He knew that Jude had everything he needed: the right ability and the right attitude. 'Trust me, he's the real deal and we've got to test him at a higher level. Just give him a chance – you'll see.'

That's what the England Under-15s manager, Kevin Betsy, had done when Jude was still only thirteen, and he had shown off his special talent straight away.

To start with, though, being selected for England had been a very daunting experience for Jude. When he first arrived at the training camp at St George's Park, he had been so nervous. Looking around at the amazing facilities and the amazing footballers, his usual confidence disappeared and the doubts crept in.

'Do I really belong here?' Jude kept thinking to himself. A lot of the others seemed to know each other already because they played together for the big Premier League clubs: Tino Livramento and Jamal Musiala at Chelsea, Cole Palmer and Taylor Harwood-Bellis at Manchester City... Yes, Jude was the stand-out star at Birmingham, but was he good enough to compete against the top kids from the top teams?

The answer was 'YES!' Once he was out on the football pitch, Jude felt more comfortable and he soon proved that he was just as brilliant as everyone else, if not even better. He quickly realised that it didn't matter what club you played for – if you're good enough, you're good enough.

At first, however, as one of the youngest members of the England squad, Jude didn't get as much game-time as he'd hoped for. Still, two twenty-minute sub appearances against Turkey was a decent start, and the training camps were a great learning experience for him. Yes, it was all worth it because a year later, when he was fourteen, Betsy had the perfect team leader in Jude, who was ready and waiting.

'Here you go,' he said, handing Jude the England captain's armband.

Wow, what an honour! He was determined to do his manager and his country proud. In their next match against the Netherlands, England won 3–1, with Jude getting two assists and his teammate Jamal getting all three goals. After knee-sliding towards the corner flag, the hat-trick hero got up to celebrate with his captain. What a deadly midfield duo they were!

So if Jude was good enough to lead England at Under-15s level, then surely he was good enough to star for the Birmingham Under-18s?

Again, the answer was 'YES!' Jude made the jump look easy and he quickly became the main man in midfield. On the ball, he showed his quality and composure, and off it, he showed his fearless fighting spirit. Although he was smaller and younger, Jude was willing to go into battle against anyone.

'Great work, Jude – keep going!' Spooner shouted encouragement from the sidelines.

And it wasn't only the Birmingham Academy coaches who were admiring Jude's ability now. The new first-team assistant manager, Pep Clotet, was so impressed by what he saw at an Under-18s match that he spoke to his boss, Garry Monk.

'That kid is incredible! We should get him training with the first team as soon as possible.'

'But he's only fourteen!' the Birmingham manager argued. 'Shouldn't we wait a few years?'

Clotet shook his head. 'Just give him a chance – you'll see.'

So one day, during a first-team training session, a taxi pulled up and a boy got out, still dressed in his school uniform. Was he there to meet the players and get their autographs? No, after getting changed into his club kit, the boy jogged out onto the pitch to join in.

'Who is this kid?' Birmingham's senior players

wondered. 'And what's he doing training with us? He looks about twelve!'

The answer soon became clear once Jude started showing off his football skills. In the finishing drill, he kept things simple and went for power at first:

BANG!... Goal! – top bins!

BANG!... Goal! – crossbar and in!

As his confidence grew, however, Jude decided to get more creative. Why not? This was his chance to shine. So the next time, he dribbled forward and faked to shoot with his right foot, but at the last second he dragged the ball back, leaving an experienced Birmingham defender lying flat on the floor. Then with his left foot, he calmly rolled the ball into the bottom corner.

Gooooooooooooooooooooaaaaaaaaaaaaaaaallllllllllllll llllllllllll!!!!!!!!!!!!!!!!!!!

'Woah, who is this kid?' Birmingham's leading striker Lukas Jutkiewicz stood there wondering.

After that, Jude began training with the first team on a regular basis. So what if he was still fourteen? As he had learned early on at England, if you're good enough, you're good enough.

As soon as he turned fifteen, Spooner decided that Jude was ready to make another massive leap – from the Under-18s to the Under-23s.

Really? Could a fifteen-year-old compete against fully-grown adults?

Again, the answer was 'YES!' On his debut against Nottingham Forest in October 2018, Jude came on as a sub and slid in bravely to score the winning goal.

'Yessssss, kid!' his new teammates cheered, chasing over to celebrate with him.

There was no stopping Jude now. In November, he led the Under-16s to the Blades Cup trophy, scoring four goals in the final against Liverpool, and then in January 2019, he scored a stunner for the Under-23s in the Premier League Cup.

As the ball bounced down on the edge of the Fulham box, Jude got to it first and dribbled forward with close control. Right, what next – shoot? No, not yet. There were too many defenders in the way, so he carried on dribbling, into the penalty area...

Now was it time to shoot? No, instead Jude fooled

four defenders with one of his clever fakes. As they all dived in front of him, he calmly switched the ball across to his left foot and curled it into the far corner.

Goooooooooooooooooooaaaaaaaaaaaaaaaaallllllllllll llllllllllll!!!!!!!!!!!!!!!!!!!!

Woah, what a moment of magic from Birmingham's bright young star! Running towards his teammates, Jude jumped up and punched the air with passion. Surely, it was only a matter of time now before his first-team dream came true?

CHAPTER 8

FIRST STEPS IN THE FIRST TEAM

But wait a minute – might Jude be moving on to a bigger club before that even happened? Following that wondergoal against Fulham, he was linked with lots of top Premier League teams, including Arsenal. So, would Jude be joining the Gunners? No, because Birmingham rejected both of their bids.

'He's not going anywhere,' the club announced.

Okay, but how were they going to keep their boy wonder happy? Jude was already training with the first team every week, so should they just hand him his senior debut straight away? No, the last thing Birmingham wanted to do was put too much pressure on him; he was still only fifteen, and he was still developing, as a player and as a person.

So instead, the club slowly started introducing him to the first team, taking things step by step:

1)   *Travelling to games with the matchday squad*

Jude enjoyed feeling like part of the team, but he wasn't there to play yet. He was just there to watch and learn about what life was like on the bus and in the changing room.

2)   *Warming up with the players*

By the end of March 2019, Jude had become Birmingham's 'nineteenth man', which meant that as well as watching, he also got to warm up with the matchday squad. Cool! As he practised his passing and shooting out on the pitch in front of the fans, he could feel himself getting closer and closer to his goal…

3)   *Going on the preseason tour*

Sadly, Jude didn't get to make his debut during the 2018–19 season, but during summer 2019, when Garry Monk was sacked as Birmingham manager, Pep Clotet took over the job. One of the first things that the Spaniard did was invite Jude on the club's preseason tour to Portugal. Yes please – wow, what an opportunity!

For their first match against Cova da Piedade, Jude started on the subs' bench, but the manager brought him on for the last thirty minutes.

'Right, here we go,' he told himself as he took a last deep breath on the touchline. 'Time to shine!'

Wearing his favourite Number 22 on the back of his shirt, Jude raced out onto the pitch and into the middle of midfield. There, he battled hard for every ball, and when the game went to penalties, he was brave enough to step up to the spot. After a fast run-up, he fired a strong shot towards the bottom corner, but unfortunately, the Cova keeper dived the right way. Saved!

Jude didn't throw his head back in despair, though; no, he just puffed his cheeks and jogged back to the halfway line. Despite his youth, he was mature enough to think, 'Oh well, I tried my best; that's all I can do.'

Jude only got to play another five minutes in Birmingham's final tour match against Vitória de

Setúbal, but a week later, back in England, he played another thirty minutes in a friendly against Swindon Town. And this time, he really took his chance to shine.

With The Blues already 4–1 up, Jude made a late run into the box, and then calmly swept the ball into the bottom corner with his left foot.

Goooooooooooooooooooooaaaaaaaaaaaaaaaaallllllllllllll llllllllllllll!!!!!!!!!!!!!!!!!!!

Ten minutes later, Jude was on the attack again. After tackling Swindon's last defender on the halfway line, he dribbled all the way into their penalty area. His first shot was saved but he managed to slide in the rebound.

Goooooooooooooooooooooaaaaaaaaaaaaaaaaallllllllllllll llllllllllllll!!!!!!!!!!!!!!!!!!!

On the sideline, Clotet clapped and smiled. What a player – the kid had so much potential! Was it finally time for Birmingham's young star to make his senior professional debut?

4)   *Playing in the League Cup*

Jude didn't make the matchday squad for any

of their first four Championship games of the new season, but for their League/Carabao Cup game against Portsmouth, there was his name, and in the starting line-up too:

22 BELLINGHAM

Hurray, what a proud moment! When he walked out onto the pitch at Fratton Park, Jude achieved not one but two of his big ambitions. Because on top of making his Birmingham debut, he had also broken Trevor Francis's record, just like he'd said he would. At sixteen years and thirty-eight days, he was the club's new youngest-ever player by a whopping 101 days!

Despite Jude's best efforts, Birmingham lost 3–0 in the Portsmouth game, but he was his team's man of the match by miles, in defence and attack. Afterwards, the club's supporters were full of praise on social media:

'Bellingham is a baller!'

'He looked class tonight.'

'He's so composed for such a young kid.'

'He's got a very bright future ahead of him.'

The fans' verdicts were positive, but what did his manager think? He agreed completely:

'I hope Jude is the one making the headlines and not the result because he is a great talent and has a big part to play in the future of our club.'

So, what was Clotet waiting for? At last it was time for Jude to take the next and final step in the first team:

5)   *Playing in the Championship*

Jude made his league debut away at Swansea City, coming on with fifteen minutes to go. What a moment! By then, however, it was too late for him to make an impact because Birmingham were already losing 3–0. Never mind, on to the next game: Stoke City at home. Jude was hoping to get maybe twenty or thirty minutes this time, but instead, he got more than sixty.

Birmingham's winger Jefferson Montero got injured in the first half, and so Clotet was forced to make an early sub. Right, who could replace him? On the bench, the Blues had lots of more experienced options: midfielders Gary and Craig Gardner, attackers Dan Crowley and Kerim Mrabti… But instead, the Birmingham manager called for his brightest young star.

'Really?' captain Harlee Dean thought to himself when he saw Jude waiting on the touchline. 'Surely, we should be bringing on someone else?'

It was a must-win match for Birmingham and they were up against a Stoke team packed with former Premier League players. At sixteen, was Jude really ready to compete against top midfielders like Joe Allen, Sam Clucas and James McClean?

Oh yes he was! Nerves, what nerves? Pressure, what pressure? As he ran out onto the pitch at St Andrew's, Jude felt no fear, only excitement. This was the opportunity he had been working towards for years, and he was determined to make the most of it.

'Yesss!'

Collecting the ball from the right-back, Maxime Colin, Jude spun cleverly away from Clucas and dribbled forward towards goal. 'Go on!' cried the fans, but unfortunately, his through-ball to Lukas Jutkiewicz was blocked.

'Unlucky, kid – keep going!' the home crowd encouraged him. They loved him already.

It was Stoke who took the lead early in the second half, but Birmingham came fighting back. First Lukas headed in the equaliser, and then they pushed forward looking for a winner. A moment of magic and a bit of luck – that's what they needed…

Pouncing on a loose ball in the middle, Jude turned and attacked the Stoke goal at speed. As he looked up, he saw Álvaro Giménez to his left and Lukas to his right, but neither was in a good position for a pass. So instead, he decided to shoot himself. BANG! It wasn't one of Jude's best strikes, but luckily it deflected off a defender's leg and rolled into the bottom corner. 2–1!

Gooooooooooooooooooooaaaaaaaaaaaaaaaaallllllllllllll llllllllllll!!!!!!!!!!!!!!!!!!!

As soon as the ball crossed the line, Jude was off, racing towards the corner flag, where he slid on his knees in front of the Birmingham fans. That morning on the way to the match, Jude had asked his parents to drive past the Bluenose rock for good luck, and look what he'd just done. What a dream home debut!

'Come onnnnn!' Jude cried out with passion in front of the Tilton Stand. This was everything he'd dreamed of as a boy and more. He really didn't want his hero moment to ever end.

CHAPTER 9

SYRENKA CUP SUCCESS

With memories of his first senior goal still fresh in his mind, Jude travelled to Poland with the England Under-17s to compete in the Syrenka Cup.

Although the tournament wasn't as big and famous as the European Championships or the World Cup, it was still a chance for Betsy's boys to test themselves against other nations and, hopefully, lift a trophy. Tino and Taylor had won it with England the year before; now it was Jude and Jamal's opportunity.

'Let's do this!' they told their talented group of teammates, including:

Strong centre-back Levi Colwill,

Skilful winger Harvey Elliott,

And sharp-shooting strikers Louie Barry and Liam Delap.

Together, they believed that they could beat anyone, starting with their first Syrenka Cup opponents, Finland.

With Jude rested on the bench, it took England thirty-eight minutes to score the opening goal. It was only when their captain came on in the seventy-first minute that everything really clicked.

After lots of neat passing, Jude got the ball in the box and fired home. 3–0!

Moments later, Louie scored from a clever free-kick routine. 4–0!

Then in the last minute, Xavier Simons finished off a flowing team move. 5–0!

'Yesssss, boys!' Jude yelled out as he walked around the pitch at the final whistle, high-fiving his teammates. So far, so good – England were off to a very exciting start.

For their next game against Austria, Jude was back in the starting line-up and at the heart of the midfield. The Young Lions really needed their leader on the pitch because after thirty minutes, they were losing 1–0.

'Come on, keep going!' Jude urged his teammates on. 'There's still plenty of time for us to turn this around!'

And they did, in the space of eight amazing minutes. Rico Richards got the first goal, Liam grabbed the second, and then Jude thumped in the third just before half-time.

'That's more like it, lads!' he shouted with a smile back on his face.

The match ended 4–2, which meant England were through to the Syrenka Cup final. There, they would face the tournament hosts, Poland.

'Bring it on!' Jude couldn't wait for the big game to kick off. What a month he was having, first with Birmingham and now with England! His confidence was sky-high and he was determined to lead his country to glory.

At the Dolcanu Stadium, the Young Lions got off to the perfect start. From inside his own half, Jude twisted and turned away from his marker and then played a perfect long cross-field pass to Harvey, who dribbled into the box and was fouled. Penalty!

Harvey got back up to take the spot-kick himself and... sent the keeper the wrong way. 1–0!

'Yesss, mate!' Jude cheered, giving their goalscorer a big hug. Wow, with less than four minutes played, England were already winning!

And six minutes later, they were celebrating again. Jamal played a one-two with the left-back James Norris, then another with Louie, before poking a shot past the keeper. 2–0!

'What a goal!' Jude shouted joyfully, as he chased after his friend. Together England's dream midfield duo were running the game.

The trophy wasn't theirs yet, though. With the home crowd cheering them on, Poland fought back. They played better and better until eventually they scored one, and then another. 2–2!

'What, how did we let that happen?!' Jude grumbled to himself as he trudged off at half-time. Oh well, England still had another forty-five minutes of football to find a winning goal...

Jude controlled the ball brilliantly and struck it sweetly on the volley, but he couldn't beat the keeper. *Saved!*

Harvey weaved his way through the Poland defence, but he couldn't beat their keeper either. *Blocked!*

Liam was the next to dribble into the box, but again, the keeper would not be beaten. Tackled!

Arggghhhh!

England's frustrations grew and grew until at last the final whistle blew. Oh well, the Syrenka Cup final would just have to be decided by a penalty shoot-out.

'Come on, you can do this!' Jude told his keeper, Coniah Boyce-Clarke. 'You're going to be our hero!'

And he was right. Coniah dived down low to save two of Poland's penalties, which meant that if Jadan Raymond could score, England would be the winners.

'Go on,' Jude muttered under his breath, looking a bit nervous for once. He was really hoping that he wouldn't have to take one himself.

When the referee blew his whistle, Jadan ran up and... smashed a shot past the Poland keeper.

Yesssssssssssssssss!

As soon as it went in, Jude was off, sprinting from the halfway line to go and hug England's heroes, Jadan and Coniah. What a feeling! The team bounced up and down together for ages in one big, happy huddle, laughing and singing.

We did it, we did it!

Campeones, Campeones, Olé! Olé! Olé!

Then once they had their medals around their necks, the England players waited for the biggest moment of all. As captain, it was Jude's job to collect the trophy and then...

Ohhhhhhhhhhhhhhhhhhhhh!

...lift it high above his head.

Hurrrrrrraaaaaaaaaaaaaayyyy!

Campeones, Campeones, Olé! Olé! Olé!

Afterwards, Jude walked around the pitch in a delighted daze. Suddenly, it felt like his football career was moving so fast. Less than two weeks after scoring his first senior goal for his club, he had just won his first trophy for his country. The first of many, hopefully.

'Syrenka Cup Winners!' Jude posted proudly on social media. 'Nice to get a couple of goals and win Player Of The Tournament. Can't wait to get back to Birmingham now.'

CHAPTER 10

BIRMINGHAM BREAKTHROUGH

Despite being captain of the England Under-17s and Birmingham's youngest-ever player, Jude refused to get carried away. No way – he had so much more to learn and so much more that he wanted to achieve. The first thing on that list was establishing himself in the Birmingham starting line-up. It was time to prove that he wasn't just a one-game wonder.

Only four days after his Syrenka Cup success, Jude took to the field against Charlton in the Championship. His first-half display was a little disappointing, but early in the second, he made his mark.

The move started with Maxime, who burst forward

on a mazy dribble up the right and then slipped the ball through to Kerim. The angle was too tight for him to shoot, so Kerim looked up and spotted Jude, unmarked in the middle, sprinting towards the edge of the box and calling for the ball.

'*Yessssssssss!*'

As the cross arrived, Jude steadied himself and then calmly slid a shot through a defender's legs and past the keeper.

Gooooooooooooooooooooaaaaaaaaaaaaaaaalllllllllllllll llllllllllll!!!!!!!!!!!!!!!!!!!!!!

Two goals in two games – Jude had done it again, and this one was a strike to be proud of! Throwing his arms out wide, he stood in front of the Birmingham fans and roared triumphantly. He was having the time of his young life.

Jude's goal turned out to be the matchwinner, lifting the Blues up to eighth in the table. Suddenly, the supporters were dreaming big. Why not? With their new wonder boy on the pitch, perhaps promotion back to the Premier League was possible!

But just like Jude himself, Pep Clotet wasn't getting

carried away. Instead, the Birmingham manager tried to take the pressure off his bright young star. Yes, he was a brilliant footballer, but at his age, he was going to have good games and bad ones. They would have to give him time to grow taller and stronger and get used to the tiring world of the Championship, where the football was very physical and teams often played two games each week.

Jude stayed in the starting line-up for Birmingham's next match against Preston, but after a 1–0 defeat, Clotet decided to move him to the bench and pick a more experienced player in the next few games.

'He needs to work to be able to play all ninety minutes,' the Birmingham manager told the media, 'and my job is to decide if he deserves to play or somebody else deserves to play.'

Yes, Boss! Every day, Jude worked hard to prove that he deserved to play the next match. This was his chance to chase his boyhood dream, 24/7, and he was enjoying every minute of it. Now that he was part of the first team, he had to grow up fast, and stay focused and professional at all times. Otherwise, he would be letting himself, and his teammates, down. Off the football pitch, he was still as humble as ever, but once he was on it, he became a different beast, full of speed and skill, courage and confidence.

'Good, Jude's on my team this time,' Harlee joked at training. 'That means we're definitely going to win!'

Jude knew that he wasn't the complete player yet, though. How could he be at sixteen years old? So, when the coaches showed him videos of ways he could improve, he always listened carefully and learned quickly. He never needed to be told something twice.

'When you're defending, you don't need to rush into every tackle. Sometimes, it's best to be patient and give your teammates time to get back into position...

...Well done – that's it, Jude!'

'We want you to be the link between midfield and attack. As soon as you get the ball, turn and go, pass and move up the pitch...

...Brilliant, lovely one-two, Jude!'

A few weeks later, Jude was back in the

Birmingham starting line-up and he stayed there
for most of the season. Sometimes, he played in the
middle as an attacking midfielder, but often Clotet
put him out on the wing. Why? Because from there,
he had the freedom to cut inside and create chances,
and if he made mistakes, it wouldn't matter so much
for the team. Plus, he had the talent to shine in any
position.

Despite Jude's best efforts, however, Birmingham
were still losing a lot of matches. In the big Midlands
derby against West Brom, Jude curled a brilliant
corner straight onto Harlee's head. Hurray, 2–1 to the
Blues! At the final whistle, however, West Brom were
the winners, 3–2.

At home against Leeds United, Jude was
everywhere. One minute, he was back in his own half
battling against Kalvin Phillips and Hélder Costa, and
the next he was sprinting forward to join the attack.
When Maxime crossed the ball to him, he took a
quick touch to control it and then calmly slotted it in
the bottom corner.

Goooooooooooooooooooaaaaaaaaaaaaaaaaalllllllllllllll

lllllllllll!!!!!!!!!!!!!!!!!!

At the final whistle, however, Leeds were the winners, 5–4. Birmingham, meanwhile, were slipping further and further down towards the relegation zone: 13th, 15th, 17th, 18th…

'Nooooo, I've got to help get us back up the table!' Jude told himself.

Although he preferred to play beautiful, passing football, he was also willing to do the ugly stuff in order to win. At home against Cardiff, the ball pinged around the six-yard box, until Jude bundled it in at the back post. 1–0!

Goooooooooooooooooooaaaaaaaaaaaaaaaaallllllllllllll lllllllllll!!!!!!!!!!!!!!!!!!

'What a feeling!' Jude posted on social media after the match. He would never, ever, get bored of scoring for his boyhood club.

Away at Barnsley, Birmingham were heading for a 0–0 draw as he chased after a long ball forward. The defenders thought that it was going out for a throw-in, but Jude didn't give up. He never gave up, no matter what. With a burst of speed, he somehow reached the ball just before it crossed the line, and then crossed it in to Scott Hogan, who swivelled and scored. 1–0!

Yesssssssssssss!

Hogan had got the goal, but really, Jude was Birmingham's hero. 'Big W,' he tweeted the next day, along with pictures of him punching the air. Yes, thanks to his tireless fighting spirit, the Blues had grabbed all three precious points to move further away from the relegation zone. Where would they be without their bright young star?

Four goals, two assists and so many magical moments – Jude was enjoying a brilliant breakthrough season, but the big question now was: how long would Birmingham be able to keep him? He was already the talk of English football and scouts from all of Europe's top clubs were watching him closely.

CHAPTER 11

SAYING GOODBYE TO BIRMINGHAM

Just weeks after Jude set up Birmingham's winner against Barnsley, the Championship season was suspended due to the coronavirus pandemic. It was a very difficult and uncertain time for everyone. How long would the lockdown last and when would it be safe to start mixing with other people again? No-one really knew.

'Stay safe everyone, see you soon!' Jude posted on social media.

He couldn't wait to get back on the football pitch, but in the meantime, he kept himself fit and busy. With all that extra time on his hands, he helped to raise lots of money for local NHS hospitals, and he also thought long and hard about his big next move.

In the January transfer window, Birmingham had rejected two bids for Jude from Manchester United – first £25 million, then £30 million – but it was agreed that at the end of the 2019–20 season, he would be saying goodbye to his beloved boyhood club. So, where would he go?

To Manchester United? When Jude visited the club with his parents, their former manager Sir Alex Ferguson even gave them a special guided tour of the training ground. Wow!

Jude, however, wasn't going to make his decision based on famous people or money. He was looking for a new club where he would feel happy, and where he would get lots of game-time. Playing football; that was what mattered most. Manchester United already had a fantastic squad and talented midfielders like Paul Pogba, Fred and Bruno Fernandes. Where would he fit in that squad, though, and would Old Trafford really be the best place for him to develop?

Jude had the same doubts about Chelsea too, who were also desperate to sign him. Their list of midfielders was long and very impressive: Jorginho, N'Golo Kanté, Mateo Kovačić, Ross Barkley, Ruben Loftus-Cheek, Willian, and then there were Frank Lampard's new young stars like Mason Mount, Billy Gilmour and Callum Hudson-Odoi.

With all that competition for places, how on earth would Jude ever get a game? That's why his good friend and England youth teammate, Jamal Musiala, had recently moved to Germany to join Bayern Munich instead.

'Mate, I love it here,' he told Jude on the phone. 'I reckon I'll make my debut this year!'

Interesting! Speaking of Germany, one of the Bundesliga's other big clubs had also made an offer for Jude: Borussia Dortmund. As well as being a top team, they were famous for giving young players a chance. Mario Götze, Ousmane Dembélé, and Christian Pulisic had all developed at Dortmund, and now the club were on to their next young superstars: Norwegian striker Erling Haaland and English winger Jadon Sancho.

Jadon was a few years above Jude in the

England youth teams, and after getting frustrated at Manchester City, he had made the bold decision to move to Germany to get more game-time. In his first season at Dortmund, Jadon had played twelve matches for the first team. In his second season, he played in forty-three, and he had even scored in the Champions League! By bravely stepping away from the Premier League, he had become one of the best young footballers in the world.

Very interesting! So, would Jude decide to follow in Jadon's footsteps? When he went to Dortmund to meet the club's directors, their message was clear: 'If you come here and do the right things, you're going to get an opportunity.'

Excellent, that was exactly what Jude wanted to hear! Dortmund became his first choice, and when the Bundesliga started back earlier than the Championship, he was able to watch their games closely.

Dortmund 4 Schalke 0:

Wow, Haaland was a beast, and the team attacked with so much pace and power!

Wolfsburg 0 Dortmund 2:

Haaland to Mahmoud Dahoud, to Jadon, to Achraf Hakimi – zoom, what a counter attack!

Dortmund 0 Bayern Munich 1:

Awww, so unlucky! Both teams had good chances to score, but Bayern were just a bit more clinical.

Paderborn 1 Dortmund 6…

By then, Jude's mind was made up: 'That's a team I really want to play for!' It was the perfect fit for him. He could see ways that he could improve Dortmund, and also ways that Dortmund could improve him.

Before he could make his big move to Germany, however, Jude had a season to finish at Birmingham. He was desperate to end things on a high, and so he carried on battling for every ball and every point for his team. Although he didn't add any more goals or assists, Jude played a key role in midfield, making lots of tackles, interceptions and accurate forward passes.

'We love you, JB – please don't leave us!' the Birmingham fans begged.

Jude loved them too, but it was time for him to take the next step. On 20 July 2020, he became a

£25 million star, the most expensive seventeen-year-old in football history.

'I'm happy to announce that I will be joining Borussia Dortmund at the end of this season,' Jude wrote on social media, with photos of him wearing his new club's yellow-and-black shirt. 'I'm very excited about this next chapter of my journey at this great club and hope to achieve many successes in the future with my new teammates and for the amazing fans!'

But first, Jude still had one last match to win for Birmingham, against a Derby County side featuring one of his biggest childhood heroes. Wow, what a moment – he was about to share a pitch with Wayne Rooney!

Jude didn't let his admiration affect his performance, though; his job was to keep the Derby captain quiet and he was determined to succeed. He followed his hero all over the field and fought hard for every ball.

'Ref!' Rooney complained when Jude fouled him, but really, the England legend was impressed. The boy clearly had the strong character needed to succeed at the highest level.

When he wasn't doing his defensive work, Jude raced forward on the attack at every opportunity. His first shot was saved, and his second flew just wide of the far post. So close! A goal would have been the perfect way to end his breakthrough season at Birmingham. But instead, after seventy-five minutes, he limped off with a knee injury. Sadly, the stadium was still empty due to COVID-19, so he couldn't even thank the supporters.

'Noooo, this is not the way I wanted to go out,' Jude kept thinking to himself, holding his shirt to his face to hide his tears.

When he went off, his team were drawing 1–1, but at the final whistle, Derby were the winners, 3–1. Oh dear, what were Birmingham going to do without their bright young star?

After the match, when everyone else had gone home, Jude went back out onto the pitch, sat down on the grass, and let the happy memories flow: his first goal against Stoke, the strike against Leeds, the wins against Middlesbrough and Nottingham Forest, the epic sounds from the Tilton Stand… Jude would miss it all so much, but it was time for him to say goodbye to his beloved Blues.

'I can't thank the club and the academy enough for what they've done for me over the last 10 years,' Jude said, ending his emotional message with a promise. 'Whatever happens Birmingham City will always be my club and I will always be a blue. It's not a goodbye it's see you later. Keep Right On!'

Birmingham weren't going to forget their local hero either. In his short spell at the club, Jude had made a massive impact with his energy, passion and entertaining style of play. So, 'to remember one of our own and to inspire others', the Blues decided to retire his Number 22 shirt.

CHAPTER 12

EARLY DAYS AT DORTMUND

'Woah!'

That was Jude's thought as he looked around at his first Dortmund training session. There was Mats Hummels, who had won the World Cup with Germany, and Marco Reus, one of Europe's most exciting forwards. He was sharing a pitch with proper football icons now.

And even the Dortmund players that Jude didn't know so well were absolutely brilliant. Left-back Raphaël Guerreiro could do all kinds of incredible things with the ball, and young attacker Giovanni Reyna looked like another superstar in the making.

'These guys are REALLY good!'

At first, it felt like a weird and wonderful dream, but Jude didn't stand there staring in awe for long. He had work to do. After a couple of relaxing weeks off, he was ready to step up and prove himself in preseason. He belonged at a big club like Dortmund, and despite his young age, he was good enough to play straight away.

'Yessss!' Jude called for the ball with confidence, before playing a clever pass through to Erling.

'That's mine!' he told himself as he raced in to make a strong tackle.

At the end of the session, Jude felt pleased with his performance, but also inspired to keep improving. His new teammates like Mats and Marco were already amazing players, and yet they still worked so hard to become even better. Jude was blown away by their desire.

'I'm going to learn so much here!' he thought excitedly.

Jude knew that it might take him a bit of time to adapt to the German style of football, which was more technical and less direct and physical than the

English Championship. However, he was sure that he had made the right decision by moving to Dortmund. He was now in the best place to become the best player he could be.

Jude also had some adapting to do away from the football pitch, though. Aged seventeen, he had just arrived in a new country, with a new language for him to learn. Fortunately, however, he wasn't making the big move on his own. For the first time ever, the Bellingham family would be split in half: Mark would stay in England to look after Jobe, who was progressing brilliantly at Birmingham, while Denise would go to Germany and live with Jude.

'I hate to think what you'd do without me,' she teased her son. 'You can't even make your bed, let alone a healthy meal!'

'Thanks, Mum – you're the best!'

Jude was also lucky to have a kind English teammate there to help him settle in. Although he hadn't known Jadon before, they quickly became good friends.

'Anything you need or don't understand, just let

me know, yeah?'

'Cheers, J!'

Thankfully, a lot of the Dortmund players and coaches could speak very good English anyway, and day by day, Jude's German got better and better too.

'I think I understood about half of that team-talk!' he told Jadon proudly.

'Nice one, bro – now you just need the other half!'

Jude's new teammates were impressed with his football skills and his language skills, but with his singing skills? Not so much. It was a club tradition that when a player signed for Dortmund, they had to stand up and perform their favourite song in front of the whole squad at dinner. Jude chose 'So Sick' by Ne-Yo and with the lyrics on his phone, he bravely got up on a chair and began. Within seconds, the room was filled with the sounds of laughter. Boy, his singing was *BAD!*

'Jude!' defender Dan-Axel Zagadou howled with delight, as Raphaël rolled around on the floor. Hmmm, maybe he should just stick to football from now on.

On the pitch, Jude was progressing really well.
He got his first Dortmund goal in a friendly against
Austria Wien and then his first assist a few days later
against MSV Duisburg.

'Great work!' his new manager Lucien Favre
congratulated him.

Dortmund's first official game of the season was in
the German Cup, and it was against Duisburg again.
So, had Jude played well enough to earn a place in
the starting line-up? Yes, there was his name and
number on the team-sheet:

22 BELLINGHAM

'Get innnn!' he cheered happily. His first chance
had arrived already, and he was determined to take it.

Jude would be playing in central midfield alongside
Axel Witsel. The Belgian was the perfect partner for
him: very experienced and very happy to sit deep and
defend. That meant Jude had more freedom to burst
forward on the attack...

When the ball bounced loose outside the Duisburg
penalty area, Jude was the first to pounce. He used his
strength to hold off his opponent and then his skill to

play a lovely pass to the left. As the cross came in, it struck the arm of a defender. Handball! Penalty!

Up stepped Jadon to score for Dortmund. 1–0!

'Yessss, J!' Jude cheered as he gave his friend a hug.

Fifteen minutes later, it was Jadon's turn to hug Jude. Giovanni's cross from the right deflected off a defender's boot and rolled out towards the edge of the box, where two Dortmund players were rushing in. Thorgan Hazard got there first, but as he was about to shoot, he heard a confident call from just behind him:

'Jude's ball!'

It was too late for Thorgan to leave it, but instead he backheeled it through for his new teammate. Jude's shot flicked up off the keeper's outstretched leg and dropped down into the net. 2– 0!

Goooooooooooooooooooooaaaaaaaaaaaaaaaaalllllllllllll llllllllllllll!!!!!!!!!!!!!!!!!!!

Jude had done it; on his debut, he had become Dortmund's youngest-ever scorer! With a focused look on his face, he pointed at his chest as if to say, 'I'm the new superstar here.'

Although Favre decided to take Jude off at

half-time, he was delighted with his youngster's complete performance:

'He attacks, he gets forward – and not just with his passing but with the ball at his feet. But he also comes back and defends with great commitment.'

Thanks, Boss! Five days later, Jude was picked to make his Bundesliga debut at home against Borussia Mönchengladbach. Could he put in another complete performance?

Yes! After thirty-five minutes of box-to-box running, the ball fell to Jude in the opposition penalty area. He seemed to be surrounded by defenders, but somehow he managed to calmly poke a pass through to Giovanni, who fired a shot past the keeper. 1–0!

Hurray, Dortmund were winning and Jude had an assist on his Bundesliga debut! It turned out the boy from Birmingham didn't need time to adapt to his new life in Germany. He was already showing his superstar quality.

CHAPTER 13

ENGLAND EXCITEMENT

After Jude had made another five Bundesliga appearances, the league stopped for an international break. He was expecting to join up with the England Under-21 squad again, for their Euro qualifiers against Andorra and Turkey, but at the last minute, there was a surprising change of plan.

The England senior team had a busy schedule with three matches in a week against the Republic of Ireland, Belgium, and Iceland. So when James Ward-Prowse and Trent Alexander-Arnold both pulled out with late injuries, the manager Gareth Southgate decided to call up an extra player to replace them:

Jude!

His family was so excited when he shared the news.

'Well done, son – we're so proud of you!'

'Bro, that's sick! Say hi to Raheem from me, yeah?'

And Jude's English teammate at Dortmund was very excited as well.

'Congrats, mate, you deserve it!' Jadon cheered. 'I told you you'd get an opportunity soon, didn't I? We're going to St George's Park together!'

At first, Jude found the whole thing hard to believe. He had only played four games for the England Under-21s so far, scoring one good goal against Kosovo. Was he really ready to step up to the seniors so soon? Everything was happening so fast. Just a few months earlier he had been playing for Birmingham in the Championship, and now look at him! He was about to train with legends like Harry Kane, Raheem Sterling, Jordan Henderson and Kyle Walker. Back in 2018, fifteen-year-old Jude had watched at home on TV as those four players and their teammates led England all the way to the semi-finals of the World Cup in Russia. Now two years later, those heroes were his new teammates!

When Jude arrived at the training camp, however, he didn't behave like a nervous little fanboy. No, he behaved like he belonged amongst England's best players. Out on the football pitch, he played like he always did – with speed and skill, composure and confidence, battling hard for every ball.

'Huge honour,' he wrote on social media once his first day was done.

Jude enjoyed testing himself against England's biggest stars in training, but what he really wanted to do was play a game for his country. The first of England's three matches, against Ireland, was only a friendly. Southgate would surely rest some of his key players ahead of the two UEFA Nations League games, so might he get the chance to make his senior international debut?

Jude wasn't named in the starting line-up, but while he sat on the subs' bench at Wembley, he was feeling hopeful about getting at least some game-time. After sixty minutes, England were already winning

3–0 – game over, time to make some changes?

Off came Tyrone Mings and on came... Ainsley Maitland-Niles.

Off came Jack Grealish and on came... Phil Foden.

Then off came Dominic Calvert-Lewin and on came... Tammy Abraham.

Oh dear, was that the end of Southgate's switches? No, ten minutes later, the manager made one more substitution. Off came Mason Mount and on came... Jude!

Yes, at the age of seventeen years and 137 days, Jude became England's third-youngest international ever, behind Wayne Rooney and Theo Walcott. But he didn't really care about that; what mattered was that he was making his senior international debut! It was his biggest football moment yet, but he didn't let his feelings show. Instead, he looked calm and focused as he high-fived Mason on the touchline and then ran onto the field to take up his position in midfield.

'Yes!' Jude called for the ball straight away.

When Harry Maguire passed it to him, his first touch was poor and he lost possession. It was a bad start, but never mind, Jude wasn't going to let one mistake affect his game. There was no time for nerves; he was determined to take his chance to shine. For the next twenty minutes, he was at the centre of everything for England. He completed every pass he attempted, including a beautiful long cross-field ball to Ainsley. He looked so comfortable out there, as if he'd been playing at this level for years. But before he knew it, the final whistle blew and Jude's senior debut was over.

'Already? I was only just getting started!' he told Jadon, who had scored England's second goal.

'Don't worry, bro – you'll be back!'

As he walked off the pitch that night, Jude slowed down to soak it all in. He was an England international now, representing his country at Wembley! Even though the stadium was empty because of COVID-19, it still had an extra-special atmosphere. Imagine how good it would feel to play there in front of 90,000 fans! Jude couldn't wait for that.

'Dream come true,' he tweeted after the game. 'It's

been some journey so far, can't wait to keep working hard and creating more moments like this.'

Jude stayed on the bench against Belgium and Iceland, but he went back to Germany buzzing about his England experience. There was no need to rush. Hopefully if he kept showing what he could do at Dortmund, he would get more chances to play for his country soon.

CHAPTER 14

CHALLENGING IN THE CHAMPIONS LEAGUE

Now that he'd made his England senior debut, Jude moved on to his next challenge: starring in the Champions League. Ever since he was a little boy, he had loved watching the tournament on TV and listening to the famous anthem, so it was a dream come true to be taking part with Dortmund.

In Dortmund's first group game against Lazio, Jude had beaten Phil Foden's record to become the youngest Englishman ever to play in the Champions League. It was so crazy – only a few months before, he had been battling in the Championship with Birmingham City!

Sadly, Jude's Champions League debut only lasted

forty-five minutes and ended in a 3–1 defeat, but his second appearance against Zenit Saint Petersburg was much more successful. Moments after coming on as a sub, he jumped high to win a header and flicked the ball on for Erling, who raced through to score. 2–0!

'Cheers, J!' Erling cheered as they celebrated the goal together.

For Dortmund's next home game against Club Brugge, Jude was back in the starting line-up and putting on a stunning midfield performance. Tough tackles, daring dribbles, perfect passes – the boy could do it all! One minute, he was racing back to clear the danger, and the next he was bursting forward to join the attack. Jude was making Europe's top club competition look easy.

Dortmund finished top of their group to set up a Round of 16 tie with Sevilla. Jude couldn't wait for their next Champions League challenge.

'that time again... #UCL,' he posted ahead of the away game in Spain.

From 1–0 down, Dortmund fought back brilliantly to win the first leg 3–2. That meant that in the second leg at home, they just had to fight hard and hold on. No problem – with Jude making lots of tackles and interceptions in midfield, they made it through to the quarter-finals. There, they would be facing... Manchester City!

Unfortunately, Jadon picked up an injury and couldn't play against his old club, but Jude was very excited about his return to England. Not only would it be a nice chance to see his dad and Jobe, but he would also be going head to head with national teammates like Kyle, Phil, Raheem and John Stones. This was what the Champions League was all about: big games against big teams.

'Let's goooooo!' He clapped and cheered as the players prepared for kick-off.

Forget Erling and Marco; in Manchester, Jude was Dortmund's most dangerous attacking player. Early on, he twisted and turned in the City box and forced Ederson to make a smart save.

'*Ohhhhhhhh!*' For a second, Jude threw his arms up in disappointment, but then he raced back into position, ready to go again.

Even when Kevin De Bruyne gave City the lead, Jude didn't let his energy levels drop. He chased after everything, including Raphaël's long pass forward in the thirty-sixth minute. Ederson rushed out to reach it first, but as he tried to control the ball, Jude stuck out a leg and stole it from him. He rolled a shot into the empty net, but...

'*FWEEEEEEEET!*' went the referee's whistle. Foul – free kick to City!

'What? No way!' Jude shouted furiously with his hands on his head. He couldn't believe it – he'd won the ball, fair and square! Instead of a first Champions League goal, he ended up with a first yellow card for arguing.

Oh well, Jude would just have to use his frustration to drive his team forward.

PING! He played a defence-splitting pass to Erling, but his shot was saved by Ederson.

ZOOM! Jude skipped away from İlukay Gündoğan and then poked another pass through to Erling, who chipped it through to Marco, who curled the ball into the bottom corner. *GOAL!*

Yesssssssss – at last, Dortmund were level! As Marco and Erling slid towards the corner flag on their knees, Jude was right behind them, diving across the slick grass.

'Come onnnnnnnnn!' he cried out with passion.

Dortmund had the away goal they wanted; now they just had to defend well and hold on for the draw. That was the plan, but in the last minute, Phil scored to win it for City.

'Nooooooooo!' Jude groaned, falling to his knees on the edge of the box. If only the referee hadn't wrongly disallowed his goal in the first half…

In that horrible moment, Jude felt absolutely gutted, but a few hours later, he was able to see the positive side. 'Still in it,' he wrote to his followers. The situation was simple: in the second leg at home at the Westfalenstadion, Dortmund had to win.

Let's gooooooooo!

As the match kicked off, Jude was feeling even more confident than usual. Why? Because four days earlier, he had finally scored his first Bundesliga goal. Away at VfB Stuttgart, Giovanni had slid the ball back to him on the edge of the penalty area. Perfect – Jude wouldn't get a better chance than this! With his first touch, he dribbled into the box, and with his second, he smashed a low shot past the keeper.

Gooooooooooooooooooooaaaaaaaaaaaaaaaaalllllllllllll llllllllllllll!!!!!!!!!!!!!!!!!!!!

So now that he had scored one, could Jude score another in the Champions League against Manchester City?

In the fourteenth minute, Mahmoud's shot was blocked and the ball bounced out to Jude, just inside the City box. He had Gündoğan behind him and Rúben Dias rushing towards him, but in that moment, it was like he had all the time in the world. With two skilful touches, Jude shifted the ball from his left foot to his right, then opened up his body and BANG! he smashed an unstoppable shot into the top corner. 2–2!

Gooooooooooooooooooooaaaaaaaaaaaaaaaaalllllllllllll llllllllllllll!!!!!!!!!!!!!!!!!!!!

Wow, what a way to score your first Champions League goal! Jude threw his arms out wide and then dived across the grass. Thanks to him, Dortmund were definitely still in the game now!

'Yessss, you hero!' Erling cheered as he jumped on Jude's back.

Unfortunately, the happy times didn't last. In the second half, City scored twice to knock Dortmund out of the Champions League. At the final whistle, Jude felt disappointed, of course, but not devastated. They had all done their best, but in the end, it just wasn't quite enough.

'The highs and lows of football,' he wrote to his fans. 'So proud to be part of this club, with these teammates.'

For Jude, there was lots to feel proud about. After a difficult start, his first season in the Champions League had turned out to be a huge success. There was now no doubt that he belonged amongst Europe's elite.

'I can't believe it, maybe he's a liar!' the City manager Pep Guardiola said after the game. 'He's so good for seventeen years old, he's a fantastic player.'

Wow, thanks Pep! 'Not bad for a Championship

player, eh?' Jude joked.

The good news for him and his Dortmund teammates was that they still had plenty more to play for. In the Bundesliga, they battled their way back up from seventh place to finish third, behind RB Leipzig and Bayern Munich. Phew!

'And breathe... Champions League, see you next season,' Jude tweeted.

And that wasn't all; Dortmund also made it through to the German Cup final. Ooooooh, was Jude about to win his first trophy as a professional footballer?

CHAPTER 15

TROPHY TIME!

13 May 2021, Olympiastadion, Berlin

'You ready for this, bro?' Jadon asked as the team bus pulled up outside the stadium, hours before kick-off.

Next to him, Jude nodded and smiled. 'You know me, mate – I'm always ready!'

Dortmund had last won the German Cup back in 2017, before either of them had even joined the club. But with Jadon and Erling both back from injury – and their big rivals Bayern Munich knocked out in the second round – they had a brilliant chance of lifting the trophy this time.

It wasn't going to be easy, though, because in the

final, they were taking on a team that had finished above them in the Bundesliga: RB Leipzig. There would be exciting battles going on all over the pitch:

Erling versus their strong centre-back Dayot Upamecano,

Jadon versus their attacking full-back Nordi Mukiele,

Mats versus their tall striker Alexander Sørloth,

And in midfield, Jude and Mahmoud versus Marcel Sabitzer and Amadou Haidara.

Let the battles begin!

In only the fifth minute, Marco tracked back to win the ball and then played it forward to Erling. He passed infield to Mahmoud, who slid it across to Jadon on the left wing.

Danger alert!

Jude watched on with excitement; he knew what was coming next. While Mukiele backed away, Jadon dribbled into the box and then with a whip of his right foot, he curled a beautiful shot past the keeper and into the far corner of the net. 1–0!

'Yesssssssss!' Jude cheered as he chased after his

goalscoring friend. What a start!

And Dortmund's domination continued. Twenty minutes later, Marco pounced on a loose pass and played the ball forward to Erling, who outmuscled Upamecano and scored. 2–0!

'Come onnnnnnn!' Jude cried out, lifting Erling high into the air.

When their young stars played this well together, they were simply unstoppable. Before half-time, Marco set up Jadon to make it 3–0. Wow, Dortmund were destroying Leipzig!

In a fantastic first half, there was only one moment that Jude wished to forget: flying into a slide tackle on Kevin Kampl after just twenty-five minutes. Yes, he sort of won the ball first, but it was still a foul.

'Arggh, why did I do that?' Jude asked himself as the referee showed him a yellow card. It was a challenge that he really didn't have to make, especially when his team was on the attack. But sometimes, he was just a bit too eager to win the ball back.

'You don't need to rush into every tackle' – that's

what his old manager Pep Clotet had told him back in his days at Birmingham City. Oh well, it was something for young Jude to keep working on. Earlier in the season, he had been sent off in the Bundesliga against Wolfsburg for two silly fouls, and Dortmund really didn't want that to happen again, especially not in the German Cup final. So the manager decided to take him off at half-time.

Although Jude was disappointed, he didn't complain. Instead, he sat on the bench, cheering his team on in the second half as they got closer and closer to glory…

'Keep going, guys!' he shouted when Dani Olmo scored a screamer for Leipzig. 3–1!

'Get innnnnnnnn!' he yelled when Jadon set up Erling on another lightning quick counter attack. 4–1!

Game over – Dortmund had done it; they had won the German Cup!

As soon as the final whistle blew, Jude raced out onto the pitch, ready to celebrate with his teammates.

Yesssssssssssssssssssssssssss!!!!!!!!!

We did it, bro!

What an amazing year! Actually, Jude had only been at Dortmund for ten months so far, and already, he was achieving his goals. Not only had he established himself as a first-team star at one of Europe's biggest clubs, but now he was also about to lift his first trophy as a professional footballer. And he was still just seventeen years old – unbelievable! All his hard work was really paying off.

Proudly wearing his winner's medal around his neck, Jude made his way up onto the stage to wait for the biggest moment of all… TROPHY TIME! It seemed to take forever, but eventually, he was surrounded by teammates and Marco was at the front with the massive gold cup in his hands.

Ohhhhhhhhhhhhhhhhhhhh…

When the Dortmund captain lifted the trophy high above his head, gold confetti filled the air, and Jude threw his arms up and roared.

Hurrrrrrraaaaaaaaaaaaayyyy!

Campeones, Campeones, Olé! Olé! Olé!

What a feeling! It was his best in football so far. Winning a major cup was everything that Jude had dreamed of as a young boy, and more. There was one thing he still needed to do, though: hold the trophy himself.

'Hey come on, it's my turn now!' Jude told Erling impatiently as he tried to give the cup another kiss.

Wow, it felt so heavy and precious in his hands! Jude didn't want to ever let go, but sadly there were other teammates waiting.

'Fiiiiiine, here you go, Gio – but be careful with it, yeah?'

Later, as the players laughed and joked on the pitch, Jude took the trophy back and posed for lots of fun photos with Jadon. Dortmund's young English stars were shining brightly together.

'Right, now I want one of just me!' Jude smiled, cuddling the cup like a child with a teddy bear.

When they finally returned to the dressing room, that's when the party really started. Mats and Jadon got up on tables to lead the Dortmund players in a big group sing-a-long that went on and on for hours. How about a rendition of 'Someone Like You' by Adele? Sure, why not? Even Jude was willing to give it a go.

He had just won the German Cup, after all!

'Special night. Special team,' he tweeted the next day.

Jude's debut season at Dortmund had been a massive success beyond his wildest dreams: forty-six games, four goals, four assists, one team trophy and one Bundesliga Newcomer of the Season award. There was no time for him to rest and reflect on his achievements, though. No, he had a busy summer ahead of him.

CHAPTER 16

A EURO 2020 EXPERIENCE TO REMEMBER

Just a week after his German Cup success, Jude headed home to England looking to lift another major trophy, this time for his country.

Since his senior international debut back in November 2020, Jude had only played the second half against San Marino, but apparently England manager Gareth Southgate had seen enough quality in those forty-five minutes. When Southgate announced England's twenty-six-man squad for Euro 2020, the list of midfielders went like this:

Declan Rice,

Jordan Henderson,

Kalvin Phillips,

Mason Mount,

And Jude!

Wow, it was another proud moment, and another dream come true.

'Yessssss, bro!' Jadon cheered when he heard the great news. 'Let's goooooooooo!'

Together, Dortmund's young English stars arrived at St George's Park full of nervous excitement for the next six weeks ahead. Could the Three Lions go from 2018 World Cup semi-finalists to Euro 2020 winners? That was the plan. At seventeen, Jude was the youngest member of the squad, but that didn't matter because everyone got on really well with each other, no matter how old they were or what club team they played for. They were all on the same team now, working together to win the same trophy.

But what would England's starting line-up be? There was so much competition for places in every position. Jadon was in a battle with Marcus Rashford, Jack Grealish, Bukayo Saka and Phil Foden for the last spot alongside Harry Kane and Raheem Sterling in attack.

And Jude? Well, Declan was a definite starter at the heart of the England midfield, leaving one place for either Jordan or Kalvin to fill. No-one was expecting young Jude to get much game-time at Euro 2020, but when had he ever let his age stop him? He believed that he was good enough to play, and there was only one way to prove it: out on the football pitch.

Jude made his first England start in their warm-up match against Austria, and he took his chance brilliantly. He looked so composed alongside Declan in midfield, and with his energy and drive, he put in an all-action performance at both ends of the pitch. In the first half, he made a great late run into the box and almost scored with a header. So close! Then early in the second half, he won the ball back near the halfway line and helped launch a quick counter attack.

Jude to Jack, to Harry, to Jesse Lingard, to Bukayo… *GOAL!*

After the match, the England manager picked out two players who had really impressed him.

'I thought both Saka and Bellingham were

excellent,' Southgate said. 'In training and matches they've played with confidence and freedom, they've played with maturity too.'

Thanks, Boss! And his teammates were really impressed too:

'The future is bright @BellinghamJude,' Jordan tweeted.

Thanks, Hendo! Jude was really pleased with the progress he was making for England, but was Euro 2020 coming a little too early in his international career? He would just have to wait and see, but the important thing was that he was...

'Ready,' Jude tweeted with happy photos of him wearing the white England shirt with his squad number on the back: 26.

For their opening game against Croatia, Southgate selected Kalvin to start alongside Declan and Mason in midfield. As Jude took his seat on the bench with Jordan, he didn't feel too disappointed. The win was the most important thing, and with ten minutes to go, they were leading 1–0, thanks to Raheem's second-half goal.

Job done? No, not quite yet. Croatia were a top team with world-class midfielders like Luka Modrić and Mateo Kovačić. So to help England hold on for the win, Southgate decided to bring on an extra midfielder of his own. But would he go for the experience of Jordan, or the energy of Jude? Off came captain Harry Kane... and on came Jude!

'Just go out there and do what you do,' his manager said, putting an arm around his shoulders.

Jude nodded back confidently, and then raced out onto the Wembley pitch, giving instructions to his teammates along the way. Aged seventeen years and 349 days, he was the new youngest man ever to play at the Euros, and the youngest man ever to play for England at any major tournament. So, was he feeling nervous? No, not at all!

Jude showed no fear and got stuck in straight away. First, he battled to win the ball against Modrić and then he jumped up and clashed heads with Domagoj Vida. Owwwww! The pain was worth it, though, because soon it was all over and England had the win they desperately wanted.

'Come onnnnnnnn!' Jude cried out, lifting his arms in front of the fans. He was already loving his Euro 2020 experience.

So, what next for England's young midfield maestro? Jude stayed on the subs bench during the 0–0 draw with Scotland, but with twenty-five minutes to go against the Czech Republic, Southgate brought him on again. The Three Lions were already 1–0 up, but another goal would help secure the victory...

'Yessssss!' Jude called out as he burst forward into the box. He was still looking for his first international goal or assist, but instead, Marcus tried to cross the ball to Jordan, and a defender blocked it.

Oh well. Was the England attack over? No, Jude never gave up, no matter what. He raced in to win the ball back and then poked it through to Jordan. GOAL!

But no, just as Jude and Jordan began to celebrate, they looked over and saw the linesman's flag was up. Offside!

Noooooooooooooooo!

Never mind, England still finished top of their group, and their next opponents, in the Round of 16, would be... their old rivals Germany! Ooooooh, what a mouth-watering clash, and on the twenty-ninth of June as well – Jude's eighteenth birthday!

Sadly, Jude himself didn't get onto the field this time, but he still enjoyed watching England win 2–0 at Wembley. When Harry Kane scored the second goal, Jude was one of the subs warming up on the touchline, and he rushed straight over to join in the celebrations.

Yessssssssssssssssssssss!

It was one big squad effort for England; they were all on the same team, working together to win the same trophy.

'Had worse presents,' Jude joked on Twitter afterwards. 'How good were the boys?'

Yes, the excitement was building all across the country because England were on fire at Euro 2020! Was football finally coming home, after fifty-five years of hurt?

Maybe, but the team still had a long way to go,

starting with a trip to Italy for their quarter-final against Ukraine. Jude got to play the last thirty minutes, but by then the match was already won.

Harry Kane slid in to score the first after only four minutes. 1–0!

Then, just after half-time, headers from Harry Maguire and, shortly afterwards, Harry Kane once again, made it three.

And just as Jude was getting ready to come on, Jordan scored his first-ever England goal. 4–0!

Although the game was pretty much over, it was still another opportunity for him to impress his manager. So Jude ran and passed and tackled and dribbled, until the referee blew the final whistle.

Yesssssssssssssssss!

Jude felt so proud to be part of such an exciting England team. 'Which way to Wembley?' he wrote later that night once the celebrations were over. 'Semis here we come.'

For the big game against Denmark, Jude was back on the bench and that's where he stayed, watching on anxiously as England fought back from 1–0 down to win 2–1 in extra-time.

Come on, come on…

YESSSSSSSSSSSSSS!

Hurraaaaaaaay, the Three Lions had done it; they were through to the Euros final! The celebrations went on long after the final whistle at Wembley, both on the pitch and in the stands. With a big smile on his face and his arms around Tyrone Mings and Reece James, Jude joined in with the full squad sing-a-long in front of the fans:

'…It's coming, FOOTBALL'S COMING HOME!'
'…SWEET CAROLINE!'

What a night! Jude really didn't want his Euro 2020 experience to end. The England team had already made history by reaching their first major tournament final since 1966. But could they go all the way and lift the trophy?

'Come on, England!'

In the final against Italy, Jude felt like a fan, supporting his teammates from the subs bench.

'Yessssssss!' he cheered as Luke Shaw scored in the second minute. 1–0!

'Nooooooo!' he groaned as Leonardo Bonucci equalised for Italy. 1–1!

Neither team could score a winner in extra-time and so the final went all the way to… PENALTIES! Despite the pain of the past, Jude believed in England's takers this time. They could do this…

1) Harry Kane… SCORED!

Yesssssss!

2) Harry Maguire… SCORED!

Yessssss!

3) Marcus… HIT THE POST!

Noooooo!

4) Jadon aimed for the bottom corner and… SAVED!

Noooooo!

The final wasn't over yet, though. Jordan Pickford made a super save to keep out Jorginho's penalty, which meant that England could equalise if they scored their last spot-kick…

5) Bukayo went for the same bottom corner as

Jadon and... SAVED AGAIN!

NOOOOO!

As he watched from the halfway line, Jude's heart sank. Now it really was over – England had lost, and Italy were the Euro 2020 winners.

Argggh, they had got so close to glory! Jude felt so gutted for himself, for the fans, the players, the coaches, but most of all, for his brave teammates who had stepped up and missed in the shoot-out: Marcus, Bukayo, and Jadon.

'Hey bro, don't blame yourself,' Jude tried to comfort his best friend from Dortmund. 'We win together, we lose together, and we'll be back!'

Jude wasn't just being nice; he truly believed that the Euro 2020 final was only the beginning for him and his talented young teammates. It wasn't to be, this time, for the Three Lions, but there was so much more to come, starting with the 2022 World Cup in Qatar.

'And by then, I'll be the main man in midfield,' Jude thought to himself determinedly.

But first, the disappointed England players trudged

forward to shake hands with Aleksander Ćeferin and collect their runners-up prizes. Jude let the UEFA President put the silver medal around his neck, but as soon as he walked away, he took it off. He would keep it, of course, but it wasn't the gold one that he really wanted. He would have to wait and see if he could win it at Euro 2024.

CHAPTER 17

BETTER AND BETTER

After his amazing Euros experience, Jude took a few weeks off to enjoy a relaxing summer holiday with his family. Ahhhhh, sunshine and swimming pools! Soon, however, it was time to return to Dortmund and get ready for season two.

'Can't wait. Let's go!' Jude tweeted happily.

It felt good to be back in Germany amongst his clubmates again, even though one very important person was no longer there by his side: Jadon. Yes, Jude's friend had gone back to England to join Manchester United for £85 million.

'Good luck, bro!'

He was really going to miss Jadon, and so would

Dortmund, but they still had Erling, Marco and Giovanni in attack, as well as a new Dutch winger, Donyell Malen. And even though Jude was still eighteen, his new manager Marco Rose decided that he was ready for extra responsibility. In his first season, Jude had played mostly as a deeper, central midfielder, but this year, Rose wanted him to get forward more often.

Yes, Boss! Jude was always looking for ways to get better and better. He wasn't the new kid at Dortmund anymore. Now he was eighteen, he was a year older, a year wiser, a year taller, and a year stronger.

'Bring it on!' he told Erling with excitement.

In the Bundesliga against Hoffenheim, Jude set up the first goal for Giovanni with a clever poked pass and then scored the second himself. As the ball flew towards him in the box, he reacted in a flash. After controlling it with his thigh, Jude then struck a left-foot shot that skipped through a defender's legs and into the bottom corner.

Goooooooooooooooooooaaaaaaaaaaaaaaaaaallllllllllll llllllllllll!!!!!!!!!!!!!!!!!!!

Jude dived across the grass towards the corner flag, and then as he got back on his feet, he punched the air with passion. By adding more goals and assists to his game, he was making a real difference for Dortmund.

A few weeks later in the Champions League, Jude was his team's attacking hero once again. When Mats played the ball out to Thomas Meunier on the right, he made his move, bursting into the gap between two Beşiktaş defenders.

'Yes, now!'

When the pass arrived, Jude chested the ball down on the run and fired a shot through the keeper's legs. 1–0!

Goooooooooooooooooooooaaaaaaaaaaaaaaaaaallllllllllllll llllllllllllll!!!!!!!!!!!!!!!!!!!!

Standing in front of the Dortmund fans, Jude threw his arms out wide and nodded his head with confidence. Yes, Jadon might have left, but now he was the team's new superstar!

Just before half-time, Jude grabbed a great assist to go with his great goal. Running onto Raphaël's long throw, he dribbled past the defender with ease and then pulled the ball back to Erling on the edge of the six-yard box. 2–0!

'Yesssssss, J!' Dortmund's new deadly duo ran towards each other and jumped up for a chest bump.

'Jude's amazing,' Erling said after his man-of-the-match performance. 'He's eighteen, three years younger than me. It's crazy.'

Now that he had the freedom to run box to box, there was no stopping Jude. He was involved in everything for Dortmund. With a driving run, he helped set up their third goal against Union Berlin, and then he slid a killer pass through for Donyell to score the winner against Sporting Lisbon. Even in games when he didn't get a goal or assist, he still played a key part for his team with his passing, tackling and endless energy.

'Step by step. Game by game. Let's keep this going!' Jude tweeted when Dortmund made it three Bundesliga wins in a row. Despite his young age, he was already acting like a leader, and he was really enjoying his extra responsibility.

When his team conceded a sloppy late goal against Mainz 05, Jude was determined to go up the other end and score. From near the halfway line, he raced forward on the attack, fighting off his marker who tried and failed to pull him back. Then just as another defender charged towards him, he slid a perfect pass across to Erling, who secured the victory for Dortmund.

'Yessssssssssssssssss!' Jude cried out as he pumped both fists at the crowd. After the match, he posted a short but powerful message on social media that summed up his winning mentality:

'Til' the end.'

And Jude's best moment of the season was still to come. Collecting Marco's pass on the edge of the Arminia Bielefeld box, he faked to shoot but dribbled between two defenders instead, and then weaved his way past another. The keeper rushed out to close him down, but that didn't bother Jude. No, he just dinked the ball over his diving body and into the net.

Goooooooooooooooooooooaaaaaaaaaaaaaaaalllllllllllll llllllllllllll!!!!!!!!!!!!!!!!!!

Woah, what a solo run, what a wondergoal, and he had made the whole thing look so easy!

Bayern Munich, beware – Jude was a man on a Bundesliga title-winning mission. With thirteen games played, Dortmund were now only one point behind the league leaders. And who was their next game against? Bayern!

It was time for Jude to send a message to an old friend and teammate: 'May the best team win, Jamal!'

CHAPTER 18

JUDE VS JAMAL

Yes, as Jude was getting better and better at Borussia Dortmund, so was his former England youth teammate Jamal at Bayern Munich. The attacking midfielder had become a two-time Bundesliga champion, as well as a senior German international. Now, the two friends were about to face each other on the football pitch in the biggest game of the Bundesliga season so far.

In the German Super Cup final back in August, it was Jamal's Bayern team that had lifted the trophy, but Jude had played well, setting up Dortmund's only goal for Marco. Four months on, he was on the best form of his life, so could he create more chances to help his team win this time?

'Come on, let's do this!' he cried out as he high-fived Erling before kick-off at home at the Westfalenstadion.

While Jamal was starting on the bench for Bayern, Jude was now one of the first names on the Dortmund teamsheet and one of their most dangerous players. In the fifth minute, he got the ball wide on the left wing, looked up, and spotted Julian Brandt making a great run through the middle.

PING! Jude's long pass was perfect, and so was Julian's skill. He twisted past Alphonso Davies and then blasted the ball past Manuel Neuer. 1–0 to Dortmund!

What a start! Their lead didn't last long, though. Bayern quickly fought back with a Robert Lewandowski goal. 1–1 – game on!

Just before half-time, Bayern scored again after some chaotic Dortmund defending, but that only made Jude even more determined. Early in the second half, the ball rolled out to him on the edge of the box. It was a golden chance, but he had to act fast. After a quick fake to shoot, Jude shifted it left to Erling, who curled the ball into the far corner. 2–2 – game on again!

'Yesssssssssssssssssssssssssssss!' Jude roared up at Erling's focused face above him. Together, they had saved the day for Dortmund.

When Jamal came on in the sixty-fifth minute, the score was still 2–2, and the match seemed to be heading for a draw. But late on, as the Dortmund keeper prepared to take a goal kick, the referee suddenly stopped play for a VAR check.

'What? Why?' Jude wondered, looking around at his teammates in confusion.

The answer was: a potential handball by Mats in his own box. After going over to watch the video footage a few times, the referee blew his whistle and pointed to the spot. Penalty!

Noooooooooooo! Jude turned away in disbelief – football could be so unfair sometimes. Up stepped Lewandowski and… 3–2 to Bayern!

And unfortunately for Dortmund, that's how it stayed, despite Jude's best efforts. At the final whistle, he fell to the grass and stared down at his feet, feeling angry and downhearted. 'There's no way we deserved to lose that!' he muttered miserably to himself. Was that the end of Dortmund's title hopes? No, Jude had to think more positively than that. There were still twenty games to go in the Bundesliga season, including a rematch with Bayern Munich.

''Til next time!' he told Jamal as they hugged and swapped shirts on the pitch. Jude even managed a tiny smile for his friend.

But by the time Dortmund arrived at the Allianz Arena in April for Round 2, they had fallen nine points behind Bayern. For all their flair going forward, they were making far too many mistakes in defence. Against a lot of teams, it didn't really matter because their amazing attackers were able to save the day: Erling, Marco, Julian, and Jude. Yes, he was a hero they relied on now – a header to equalise against Eintracht Frankfurt, an assist for Erling against Freiburg...

But against Germany's top teams, Dortmund couldn't get away with their dodgy defending. They had already lost 4–1 against RB Leipzig and 5–2 against Bayer Leverkusen. Uh-oh, what was going to happen against the best opponents of all, Bayern Munich?

By half-time, Dortmund were already 2–0 down – two mistakes, two goals.

'This can't keep happening!' Jude screamed angrily, blasting the ball in frustration.

But it did. Late on, their defenders failed to clear the ball away and who was there to score Bayern's third? Jamal!

'Offside!' Jude argued, but no, the linesman's flag stayed down.

Soon, it was all over. Dortmund had been beaten and Bayern Munich were the Bundesliga Champions… again.

'Congrats, mate,' Jude hugged Jamal, hiding his own disappointment for a moment. Despite all his goals, assists and all-action performances, his second season at Dortmund was going to end without a trophy.

Oh well, on to the next one, and the Jude vs Jamal

battle was far from over. Because in the UEFA Nations League, England had been drawn in a group with Italy, Hungary... and Germany!

'May the best country win!'

For the first match in Munich, Jude started on the bench, but in the fourteenth minute, Kalvin had to go off with an injury and on he came, ready to fight hard for his country. One minute, he was flying into a tackle to win the ball back, and the next he was racing forward to join the attack. He even got a goalscoring chance, but his shot was blocked by Antonio Rüdiger.

Ohhhhhhhhhhhhhh!

It was Germany who took the lead early in the second half, but England came fighting back. Raheem passed it to Jack Grealish on the left, who curled a brilliant ball across the six-yard box to Harry Kane. Surely, he was about to score, but no, his shot was saved.

Noooooooooooooooo!

As the England captain lay there on the grass with his head in his hands, Jude rushed over to help him back up. 'Keep going, H – the goal is coming!'

What a young leader he was, and he was right about the goal. Ten minutes later, Harry was tripped as he turned in the box, and scored from the penalty spot. 1–1!

Yesssssssssssssssss!

The first Jude vs Jamal international had ended in a hard-fought draw, but would there be a winner in the return match at Wembley?

This time, with Kalvin still out injured, Jude was in the England starting line-up, and so was Jamal for Germany. It was a massive match for both teams because it was their last chance to impress before the 2022 World Cup in Qatar.

'Come onnnnn!' Jude clapped and cheered as he took up his position next to Declan in midfield.

After a dull first half, the game suddenly came alive in the second, but it was bad news for England. First, Jamal was fouled by Harry Maguire as he dribbled into the box, and İlukay Gündogan scored from the penalty spot. Then fifteen minutes later, Kai Havertz had far too much time and space to curl a long-range shot into the top corner. 2–0!

Uh-oh, a loss to Germany in their last game before the World Cup – what a disastrous defeat it would be for England! Jude was determined to stop that from happening. As soon as he got the ball, he drove his team forward and then passed to Reece James on the right, who played a one-two with Bukayo before crossing it to Luke Shaw at the back post. 2–1!

Game on! Four minutes later, Bukayo dribbled through the Germany defence and set up Mason to score the equaliser. 2–2!

'Yessssss, let's win this now!' Jude shouted as the England players celebrated.

With ten minutes to go, Bukayo turned and tried to slip a pass through to Jude, who was just inside the Germany box. But as Jude stretched out his leg to reach the ball first, a defender caught him painfully on the shin.

'Argggghhhhh!' he cried out in agony on the ground.

At first, play carried on, but eventually, after a VAR check, the referee did award a penalty to England, which Harry Kane coolly fired past Neuer. 3–2!

'Come onnnnnnnnnnnnn!' Jude roared, pumping his fists at the England fans above. What a comeback, and he had played a really crucial part!

The game wasn't over yet, though. Nick Pope couldn't hold on to Serge Gnabry's late swerving strike and the ball spilled out to Havertz. 3–3!

'Noooooooooo!' Jude groaned as his shoulders slumped and his head dropped. After all that hard work!

The second Jude vs Jamal international ended in another draw, but at least it had been a very exciting match. And for England, there were some major positives ahead of the World Cup. Bukayo had been brilliant on the right wing, and Jude had been sensational in central midfield. After his Player-of-the-Match performance, all of the TV pundits were talking about him, and for once they all agreed:

'England need to build a team around Jude Bellingham.'

CHAPTER 19

ANOTHER SEASON, ANOTHER STEP FORWARD

Back in Germany, Dortmund were also looking to build a team around Jude. It had been a busy summer for the club, with Erling and Manuel Akanji both moving to Manchester City, and Axel signing for Atlético Madrid. Replacing them were defenders Niklas Süle and Nico Schlotterbeck, midfielder Salih Özcan, and exciting young forward Karim Adeyemi.

It all meant that Jude was now Dortmund's number one superstar, as well as one of the senior players in the squad. In fact, when it came to selecting his captains for the 2022–23 season, the new manager Edin Terzić went for:

1) Marco,

2) Mats,

and

3) Jude!

Wow, really? 'He's the oldest nineteen-year-old I've ever seen,' Terzić explained.

Thanks, Boss! Jude couldn't wait to take another step forward and become even more of a leader for his club.

'A captain already – proud of you, bro!' Jobe said with a smile when he heard the news. Back in England, the younger Bellingham was flying through the ranks at Birmingham City, just like his big brother – Under-18s, then Under-23s and now, aged sixteen, in the first team. Sadly, Jude had missed Jobe's senior debut, but he had a good excuse – he had been playing for Dortmund at the same time.

'Hey, proud of you too, bro!' Jude replied. 'But leave my Birmingham records alone, yeah?'

'Well, we'll see about that...'

As the new season kicked off, the big question at Dortmund was: with Erling gone, where would their goals come from?

In the first round of the German Cup against 1860 Munich, the answer was:

1) Donyell,

2) Jude,

and

3) Karim

'Win and a goal to get things started,' Jude tweeted afterwards.

Dortmund started well in the Bundesliga too, with battling wins over Bayer Leverkusen and Freiburg. So far, so good! Jude was enjoying his new role as a more experienced member of the team.

'My sons,' he joked about a photo of him with Dortmund's next big things, Youssoufa Moukoko and Jamie Bynoe-Gittens.

With so many young players, though, there were always going to be ups and downs for the new Dortmund. They lost to Werder Bremen and RB Leipzig in the Bundesliga, but in the Champions League, their senior stars really stepped up and showed their class.

Marco scored Dortmund's first goal against FC

Copenhagen, followed up by Raphaël, and then
Jude with a stylish side-foot finish. Job done! Next,
Dortmund faced Manchester City, and their old
friends Erling and Manuel. City were the favourites to
win, especially at home, but early in the second half,
Jude cleverly flicked on Marco's cross to give his team
the lead.

*Goooooooooooooooooooaaaaaaaaaaaaaaaallllllllllll
lllllllllllll!!!!!!!!!!!!!!!!!!!!*

Jude stood there in front of the fans for a long time
with his arms out wide, enjoying his hero moment.
What a big-game player he was!

He wasn't the only one, though. City fought back
and Erling ended up scoring a spectacular winner.

'Noooooooooooo!' Jude groaned as he turned
away, shaking his head with frustration. Yet again,
Dortmund had played well against a top team, but not
quite well enough.

Oh well, on to the next match against Sevilla, and
it was all set to be a very special one indeed. With
Marco and Mats both out injured, Jude was the new
number one team leader. He had already captained

Dortmund in the Bundesliga against FC Köln, and now, he was about to wear the armband in the Champions League too. Wow, what an honour!

When the game kicked off, Jude didn't go around shouting and screaming at his teammates; no, that wasn't his style. Instead, he led by example, and he led Dortmund to victory.

In the fifth minute, Jude got the ball, looked up and floated a perfect long pass out to Raphaël on the left. After cutting inside, Raphaël fired a rocket of a shot past the Sevilla keeper. 1–0!

'Yesssssss, Rapha!' Jude cheered, throwing his arms up in the air as he raced towards his teammate.

And that was just the start for Dortmund. Just before half-time, Jude burst forward from midfield, pointing to the space in front of him. When the pass arrived from Salih, he dribbled forward, twisted and turned away from the defender, and then poked a shot into the bottom corner. 2–0!

Goooooooooooooooooooooaaaaaaaaaaaaaaaaaalllllllllllll llllllllllllll!!!!!!!!!!!!!!!!!!!!

The run, the skill, the finish – woah, what a

special, solo goal! This time, Jude didn't go over to the supporters to celebrate like usual. Instead, he raced over to the bench to celebrate with his manager.

'Thanks for believing in me, Boss!' he shouted, giving Terzić a big hug.

At the final whistle, Dortmund were 4–1 winners and the players bounced up and down together in front of the fans. Thanks to his goal and assist, Jude got the man-of-the-match award too, to go with the captain's armband. It was a night that he would never forget.

And a week later in the home game against Sevilla, Jude was at it again. With his team losing 1–0, he raced forward and volleyed in from Thomas Meunier's cross. 1–1!

Goooooooooooooooooooaaaaaaaaaaaaaaaalllllllllllll llllllllllll!!!!!!!!!!!!!!!!!!

Four in four games – Jude really loved the Champions League! And he was banging in the goals in the Bundesliga too. After losing to Union Berlin, Jude was determined to help get Dortmund back on track against Stuttgart. In only the second minute of the match, he got the ball on the edge of the box and passed it right to Niklas, who played it back for the one-two. With a classy swing of his foot, Jude swept the ball into the net. 1–0! Simple! He had the talent to make football look so easy.

By half-time against Stuttgart, Dortmund were already 3–0 up, and early in the second half, Jude scored again with a goal that showed off all his strengths:

The determination to win the ball back,

The skill to spin and escape from his opponent,

And the confidence and accuracy to curl a shot into the bottom corner.

Goooooooooooooooooooaaaaaaaaaaaaaaaalllllllllllll llllllllllll!!!!!!!!!!!!!!!!!!

What a superstar! And now that he'd started scoring, he couldn't stop. A week later against Frankfurt, Jude raced on to Youssoufa's pass, cut inside the last defender, and finished in style to win the game for his team. Dortmund's top scorer was up to nine goals for the season already!

More goals, more responsibility – Jude was just

getting better and better. And as ever, his timing was perfect because the 2022 World Cup in Qatar was now only weeks away...

CHAPTER 20

ENGLAND'S WORLD CUP WONDERKID

On 10 November 2022, just ten days before the World Cup kicked off, Southgate announced his England squad at last. For some, it had been an anxious wait, but not really for Jude. After his player-of-the-match performance against Germany and all those goals for Dortmund, he was feeling confident that his name would be there amongst the twenty-six players. And it was!

Midfielders: Jude Bellingham (Borussia Dortmund)…

Hurray, he was in; he was going to Qatar! It was another incredibly proud moment for Jude and his whole family.

'One of my biggest dreams growing up was to play at a World Cup,' he posted on social media. 'I'm so grateful to have been given the chance to do so. Will give everything to try and make it a tournament that the country can be proud of. Let's go.'

Euro 2020 had been an amazing experience for Jude, even if he hadn't got to play as much as he'd hoped. Now, at his second major international tournament, was he ready to step up and be England's main man in midfield? Oh yes, with Kalvin still recovering from injury, Jude was determined to secure a starting spot alongside Declan.

When the squad set off for Qatar, the team spirit was as strong as ever. Jude really felt like one of the England lads now, and he had made so many good friends: Bukayo, Reece, Trent Alexander-Arnold, Jordan, Phil, Ben White... the list went on and on. Jude even got on well with Jack Grealish, who was a big fan of Birmingham City's local rivals, Aston Villa.

'Hey, we're just two Brummie boys playing for the same team now!' they agreed.

After a tough week of training and getting used

to the hot, humid weather, it was time for England's World Cup adventure to begin against Iran. So, who would Southgate select in the starting line-up? The answer was:

Bukayo in attack alongside Harry and Raheem, and in midfield – Declan, Mason... and Jude!

Hurray! On his World Cup debut against Iran, Jude took a little while to settle into the game, but once he did, he made a massive difference for England with his excellent runs from midfield. As Luke Shaw curled in a cross from the left, Jude sprinted towards the six-yard box to meet it. Then calmly and cleverly, he guided his header into the corner of the net. 1–0!

Gooooooooooooooooooooaaaaaaaaaaaaaaaaalllllllllllll llllllllllllll!!!!!!!!!!!!!!!!!!!!

Hurray, England were winning and Jude was their hero! As the crowd roared, he leapt high into the air, raising his right fist to the sky. What a time to score his first senior international goal – on his World Cup debut!

Now that Jude had shown the way, the England goals kept on coming.

Bukayo fired in from the edge of the area. 2–0!

Then just before half-time, Jude dribbled forward from the halfway line, and passed the ball to Harry, who crossed it to Raheem. 3–0!

In the second half, Bukayo scored again, then Marcus Rashford came on to make it five, and finally, with just minutes to go, Jude burst forward once again and passed the ball through to Callum Wilson, who cut it back for Jack. 6–1!

What a performance and what a start to the World Cup! At the final whistle, the England players celebrated an impressive 6–2 victory. While it was Bukayo who collected the Player-of-the-Match award, Jude must have been a very close second after his great goal and two key passes. Everyone was very excited about England's new midfield maestro, but Jude wasn't getting carried away. The win was the most important thing, and it was only the first step in what was, hopefully, going to be a long World Cup journey.

'Start as we mean to go on,' he tweeted afterwards. 'Let's keep pushing!'

Their next match against the USA, however, turned out to be a very different kind of game. Early on, Jude managed to burst forward and help set up a chance for Harry, whose shot was deflected wide. But after that bright start, England struggled to find another way through the American midfield. Instead of attacking, Jude spent most of his time defending, and after seventy frustrating minutes, he was subbed off.

Oh well – although a 0–0 draw was a bit disappointing, it wasn't that bad. England just needed to beat Wales now, and they would still finish top of Group B.

This time, Southgate decided to make some changes to the starting line-up, but it was Mason who moved to the bench, not Jude. Phew! Suddenly England's midfield three looked a lot more balanced, with Declan and Jordan doing the defensive work, and Jude joining the attack at every opportunity.

'Yes!' he called out as he raced forward to collect Harry's pass, and then he played the ball through to Kyle Walker with a beautiful flick.

Olé!

Jude carried on running for the one-two, and when it arrived, he dribbled into the Wales box and backheeled it to Phil, whose shot flew just over the bar.

'Unlucky!' Southgate cheered from the sidelines. What a goal that would have been!

At half-time, it was still 0–0, but early in the second half, England got the goals they deserved. First, Marcus curled an unstoppable free kick into the far corner, and then a minute later, Harry fizzed the ball across the six-yard box, and there was Phil rushing in at the back post. 2–0!

'Yesssssss, mate!' Jude shouted joyfully as he wrapped his arms around his teammate in front of the fans. England were enjoying themselves now. In the sixty-eighth minute, Marcus scored again to make it 3–0, and before the final whistle, Jude had a great chance to grab a fourth. The pass from Callum was perfect, but his shot wasn't powerful enough to get past the keeper. Saved!

Noooooooo! Never mind, the main thing was that England were on their way through to the knock-

outs. Next up, in the Round of 16: Senegal. Even
without their injured star player, Sadio Mané, the
African Champions were still going to be a tough
team to beat. In fact, for the first thirty minutes,
Senegal were the better side, but eventually, England
got back into the game, thanks to their excellent
midfielders.

As soon as Harry got the ball near the halfway line,
ZOOM! Jude was off, racing into the space behind the
Senegal defence. When the pass arrived, he had three
defenders chasing back behind him, and one defender
in front of him, but Jude didn't panic. He dribbled
on into the box, looking for support, and then at the
crucial moment, just when it looked like his chance
might have gone, Jude slipped a sublime pass between
two defenders, and across to Jordan. 1–0!

'Come onnnnn!' Jordan cried out, first pointing
at Jude and then running straight towards him. After
going head-to-head for an intense moment, they
hugged each other with passion. What an important
goal they had just scored together!

And just before half-time, Jude helped England to

score another. Rushing in to win the ball back just outside his own penalty area, he dribbled forward, battling his way past one defender. Now what? Looking up, Jude passed the ball left to Phil, who passed it to Harry on the right. He was one on one with the keeper – surely he had to score? Yes. 2–0!

After the final whistle, Jude was all smiles as he sat on the pitch, making a 'W' with his hands for the cameras. He had certainly achieved his aim of becoming England's main man in midfield. Another game, another two key passes, another amazing, all-action performance – what a wonderful World Cup he was having!

'There's no weakness in his game,' Harry, his captain, praised him after the match. 'He's full of energy, he's great on the ball, he scores goals, he got an assist today… he's a really talented player.'

Thanks, H! And Jude's fellow midfielder went even further. When asked about him, Jordan started with a one-word answer: 'Incredible'. 'I can't keep saying nice things about him,' he continued. 'We're talking about, for me, a one-off.'

Wow, thanks, Hendo! Jude was an England hero now, and hopefully, there would be many more match-winning moments to come, starting with their quarter-final against the reigning World Champions.

CHAPTER 21

WORLD CUP WOE

10 December 2022, Al-Bayt Stadium

Yes, two of Europe's top teams, England and
France, were going head to head in the World Cup
quarterfinals – what an entertaining battle it was
going to be! All over the pitch, there were match-ups
to look out for:

Harry Kane vs Dayot Upamecano,

Harry Maguire vs Olivier Giroud,

Bukayo vs Theo Hernández,

Kyle vs Kylian Mbappé,

Declan vs Antoine Griezmann...

...and Jude vs another bright young midfield

maestro, Aurélien Tchouameni of Real Madrid.

'Bring it on!' Jude thought to himself as the teams walked out onto the pitch for kick-off. He had always been a confident kid, but now after his star performances against Iran and Senegal, he felt like he could win any battle and any match for his country.

Beating France, however, was going to be England's toughest task yet. After an even start, the first goal arrived in the seventeenth minute. It all began with Bukayo on the attack. As he tried to twist and turn away from Upamecano on the right wing, the defender tripped him up.

'Foul!' the England players cried out, but the referee said no. Play on!

What?! But there was no time to argue because France were on the counter-attack...

Although Jude raced all the way back to his own box to defend, he couldn't quite block Tchouameni from blasting a stunning shot into the bottom corner. 1–0!

But despite that early setback, the England players didn't let their heads drop. Instead, they pushed forward positively, looking for an equaliser.

Harry Kane turned brilliantly in the box, but he couldn't poke a shot past Hugo Lloris, and on the rebound, Jordan's cross floated just over Jude's head.

Oooohhhhhhhhhhhhhhhhh!

Moments later, Harry had the ball in the France box again, and this time, he fell to the floor after another clumsy tackle from Upamecano.

'Penalty!' Jude and his teammates screamed, throwing their arms in the air, but again, the referee said no.

'No way, ref – that's another foul!'

Even though it felt like all the big decisions were going against them, England battled on brilliantly. As usual, Jude was working hard at both ends of the pitch. One minute, he was back helping Kyle to stop Mbappé, and the next he was forward in the France box, calling for the cross. Harry decided to go for goal instead, though. His long-range strike dipped and swerved, but it didn't beat Lloris.

Unlucky, keep going!

Come on, England!

At half-time, it was still 1–0, but just after the break, another big chance arrived for England. Phil's corner kick was cleared to the edge of the area, where Jordan beat Mbappé to the bouncing ball and knocked it across to Jude. There was no time or space to think; he just had to hit it first time. *BANG!* His right foot connected beautifully with the ball and it flew like an arrow towards the top corner… but somehow Lloris sprang up and flicked it over the bar.

'Noooooooooooooo!' Jude groaned, holding his face in shock and horror. He had just come so close to being his country's hero again.

Five minutes later, however, England did get the goal they deserved. As Bukayo dribbled up the right wing, Jude made another bursting run from midfield. 'Yessss!' When the ball came to him in the box, Jude could sense a defender behind him closing in, so he cleverly flicked it back to Bukayo for the one-two. Bukayo tried to create enough space for a shot, but he was fouled by Tchouameni.

'Penalty!' the England players cried out again, and this time, the referee said yes.

'Come onnnnnnnn!' Jude roared, pumping his fists at the fans, and his celebrations were even louder a minute later when Harry scored from the spot. 1–1!

Game on! The next goal was going to be key, but who would score it?

Adrien Rabiot? No, his shot was saved by Jordan Pickford.

Harry Maguire? No, his header flew just wide of the post.

Oooohhhhhhhhhhhhhhhhh!

Unfortunately for England, the next goalscorer turned out to be Giroud, with a clever glancing header. 2–1 to France!

When the ball landed in the net, some of the England players threw their hands to their heads in despair, but not Jude. He never gave up, no matter what. There were still at least fifteen minutes to go – plenty of time to grab another equaliser...

When Jude got the ball near the halfway line, he looked up quickly and spotted Mason on the move. *PING!* His long pass was perfect, but as Mason tried to control it, he was barged over in the box.

'Penalty!' Jude and his teammates screamed again, but again, the referee said no. Well, at first, anyway. When VAR told him to check the replays, however, he changed his mind and pointed to the spot.

Yesssssssssssssssssssssssss!

This was it; England's chance to equalise. As Harry stepped up to take it, he looked as calm as ever, but with the pressure on, he went for too much power and blazed it over the bar.

Noooooooooooooooooooo!

It was a massive miss at a crucial moment, but as Harry stood there alone and devastated, one of his teammates rushed over to comfort him. Guess who? Yes – Jude, England's youngest player.

'Come on, you can still win us this game!' he urged his captain on.

But despite Jude's encouraging words, it just wasn't England's night. After one last free kick from Marcus, the final whistle blew, and France were the winners, going through to the World Cup semi-finals.

England, meanwhile, were out. As the news sunk in, Jude collapsed on the grass, with tears streaming down his face. He had wanted to win the World Cup so badly, and it was a match they really didn't deserve to lose. In the end, it took two of his teammates, Kalvin and Conor Coady, to lift him back up.

'This one will be painful for a very long time,' Jude posted the day after England's exit. 'The better team on the night went out, that's football sometimes.'

It wasn't all doom and gloom, though. The Three Lions had narrowly lost to the World Champions in a hard-fought battle, and they would all learn a lot from the experience, especially the younger players. Bukayo, Marcus and Phil had all been brilliant in attack, while in midfield, Declan and Jude had both been magnificent.

What a rapid rise it had been for Jude. In just two years, he had gone from the Championship to the Champions League, and from a sub at the Euros to a World Cup superstar. Tackling, running, dribbling, passing, shooting – the boy from Birmingham could do it all, and he did it with such energy, determination, and will to win. Yes – with a world-class nineteen-year-old leader like him, the future looked very bright indeed for England.

Jude ended his emotional message with a promise to the fans, and to himself: 'Keep the faith, our time will come.'

BELLINGHAM HONOURS

Borussia Dortmund
🏆 DFB-Pokal: 2020–21

England Under-17s
🏆 Syrenka Cup: 2019

Individual
🏆 Syrenka Cup Player of the Tournament: 2019
🏆 Birmingham City Young Player of the Year: 2019–20
🏆 EFL Young Player of the Season: 2019–20
🏆 VDV Bundesliga Newcomer of the Season: 2020–21
🏆 VDV Bundesliga Team of the Season: 2021–22
🏆 IFFHS Men's World's Best Youth Player: 2022
🏆 Bundesliga Player of the Year: 2022–23

BELLINGHAM

22 **THE FACTS**

NAME: Jude Bellingham

DATE OF BIRTH: 29 June 2003

PLACE OF BIRTH: Stourbridge

NATIONALITY: English

BEST FRIEND: His brother Jobe

CURRENT CLUB: Real Madrid

POSITION: Central Midfield

THE STATS

Height (cm):	186
Club appearances:	192
Club goals:	42
Club assists:	30
Club trophies:	1
International appearances:	27
International goals:	2
International trophies:	0
Ballon d'Ors:	0

★ ★ ★ **HERO RATING: 88** ★ ★ ★